PRAISE FOR *THE FAIR WAY*

"In THE FAIR WAY, Birgit Koebke and Kendall French take us on a journey that is both deeply personal and universally important. This book will inspire anyone who believes in the power of showing up and speaking out. Let it spark change."

—**BILLIE JEAN KING**, Sports Icon and Equality Champion

"B. Koebke and Kendall French stood strong in the face of injustice, demanding equal treatment as an unmarried, same-sex couple. With fortitude and dignity, they fought for their rights and, in doing so, set a powerful legal precedent requiring businesses to treat domestic partners equally to married couples. This illuminating and gripping account of their journey is sure to inspire others to stand up for the justice and respect we all deserve."

—**JON W. DAVIDSON**, Senior Counsel, ACLU Foundation

"Over two decades ago, I covered the story of two courageous women fighting for equality in the face of relentless opposition. THE FAIR WAY is their candid and powerful true story—a decade-plus-long battle that led to a landmark case for equality. Their fight was as inspiring as it was hard-fought, and the impact of their victory still resonates today. This story has never been more relevant, serving as both a testament to perseverance and a reminder of the work still to be done."

—**ARMEN KETEYIAN**, 11-time Emmy award winner and six-time NYT bestselling author

"THE FAIR WAY **is a testament to the many forms servant leadership can take. B.** *Koebke and Kendall French's commitment to justice goes beyond their own fight, furthering the cause of so many others. Their courage, resilience, and dedication to fairness serve as an inspiring reminder that true leadership is about lifting others up. A compelling and important read!"*

—**KEN BLANCHARD**, NYT bestselling coauthor of *The One Minute Manager®* **and** *Leading at a Higher Level*

"THE FAIR WAY invites readers to join B and Kendall on their journey from golf clubhouse to California's highest courthouse, along the way meeting fair-weather friends and stubborn prejudice before the satisfaction of helping to bend the long arc of the moral universe toward justice. Theirs is an engaging story of two women in love with each other and with the fun and camaraderie of golf. They simply asked for fairness but had to persevere through years of rejection before achieving their high-profile court victory and ultimate vindication. Then, with love and determination having carried them through, they came full circle, returning to warm welcomes from new and old friends in their original clubhouse. Lambda Legal was proud to represent them in securing their legal breakthrough that helped pave the way for marriage equality."

—**JENNIFER C. PIZER**, Chief Legal Officer and Eden/Rushing Chair, Lambda Legal

THE FAIR WAY

The True Story of a Landmark Case for Equality

B. BIRGIT KOEBKE

KENDALL FRENCH

FAIR WAY PUBLISHING
SAN DIEGO, CA

THE FAIR WAY is a work of nonfiction. The events and conversations from this book are a reflection of the authors' experiences, best recollections, and inferences. Some names have been altered to honor the privacy of those involved.

Edited by Shelley Chung and Jared Kuritz
Proofread by Cindy Doty
Cover and Interior Design by Gwyn Flowers, gkscreative.com

Publishing & Media Inquiries:
STRATEGIES Public Relations
PO Box 178122
San Diego, CA 92177

ISBN: 979-8-9926432-0-6 (IngramSpark Trade Paperback)
ISBN: 979-8-9926432-1-3 (KDP Trade Paperback)
ISBN: 979-8-9926432-2-0 (ebook)

FIRST EDITION

First Printed in the United States.

First Published in the United States by Fair Way Publishing

DEDICATION

This book is dedicated to Jon W. Davidson and Marcia Chambers.

Jon is a true gentleman, an exceptional litigator, and an extraordinary human being. Without his unwavering drive for fairness and equality, our victory—and the preservation of dignity—would not have been possible.

Marcia was our lifeline, thrown to us when we felt adrift in turbulent seas. The timing of her article in *Golf for Women* was a pivotal moment, serving as both a catalyst and a beacon that gave our story national visibility.

We will always be deeply grateful to these two remarkable individuals.

TABLE OF CONTENTS

Introduction

The story you are about to read is true to the best of our recollection. Out of respect for the privacy of certain individuals, some names were changed. As with our approach to this ordeal, and our journey through life, we wrote this book together.

As a comparatively civil society, change is a necessary and inevitable part of progress. Sometimes change comes naturally and smoothly through common ground and the greater good. And sometimes it must be constituted in a more vigorous manner through new laws, civil disobedience, and even force. Change can come about slowly through many years of small steps, or it can be more immediate and abrupt. Regardless of the manner in which it comes about, there will always be people on both sides of the fence—and you will likely be surprised about where some of your friends and family members fall.

We did not set out to effect significant changes in social policy or massive changes in the law. We did not have the slightest expectation or thought that our seemingly fair and innocuous personal request would lead to a seven-year landmark legal battle that had the potential to impact the lives of hundreds of thousands of people. In fact, had we known our minor request was going to send us down the path it did, we might not have taken up the fight.

The words *activist* and *confrontational* seldom if ever have been used to describe either of us. But given the length of this battle and the toll it took on us emotionally, socially, and financially, we're often asked three common questions: Why did we engage in the fight? Why didn't we just move to a more accepting and inclusive situation? Given what we went through, would we do it again?

So why did we take up this fight? The answer is not complicated—we didn't look for this fight at all. In fact, we proactively did everything we could to avoid it without compromising our own principles. But when we reached the point where we knew we would have to either escalate this to a legal battle or walk away, the decision was a lot easier than we expected. Not everyone has the opportunity to stand up to injustice and fight for what is right. We felt that because we had the means, resources, and fortitude to do so, it was our responsibility. We never imagined this would turn into a groundbreaking case that paved the way for so many others. But we are grateful it did.

It's true, we could have taken the path of least resistance and simply walked away. But Bernardo Heights Country Club was our club. It was where we wanted to be. We had developed friendships. To us, it was a second home. It was the club's unfair and discriminatory policy with which we took issue.

This fight monopolized seven years of our lives, cost us a significant amount of money and countless friends, and most certainly added stress and tension to our lives. The frustration we felt was indescribable when you consider that, from day one, the solution we had offered would have been free.

Would we do it again? Absolutely. This case is our legacy.

For us, writing this book has been a cathartic way to reflect upon the enormity of what we experienced and what we were able to accomplish. We hope it inspires you to take action if the opportunity to correct an injustice presents itself to you one day.

This is our story.

B. Birgit Koebke and Kendall E. French

CHAPTER ONE

California State Supreme Court

May 2005

Sitting in the California Supreme Court's main courtroom in San Francisco waiting for the seven justices to enter and hear their case was one of the most surreal moments of B. Birgit Koebke's and Kendall French's lives. We hear that being in court is nothing like what we see on TV. Most of the time, this is probably true. But on this occasion, the couple's case was about to be heard by the most powerful and influential state court in the country, which would render a decision affecting the personal lives of hundreds of thousands of people and countless industries.

The room was quiet except for the shuffling of papers and murmured conversations among the two parties preparing to make their arguments. The solid wood doors at the main entrance in the back of the room opened occasionally as a member of the media or other interested person entered and took a seat to observe the proceedings.

B and Kendall sat up in the gallery and watched as their attorneys huddled around a rectangular table some ten feet from the base of the justices' five-foot-high, crescent-shaped raised bench. The bench was an imposing structure that represented the power and influence of the people who occupied its seven high-backed chairs. It spanned at least thirty feet, allowing each justice an ideal view of the room. Behind it was a twelve-foot-high wall that matched the bench in style and breadth. Panning upward, the backdrop was finished with an equally broad, eight-foot-tall mural of a scenic California landscape—a valley with a river that led to a grand mountain range in the distance. The top of the arched mural met the curve of the vaulted ceiling.

A heavy combination of excitement, anxiety, and fatigue underscored the gravity of this moment for B and Kendall. It was the culmination of a seven-year battle that had consumed their lives, cost them friends, and tested their resolve. From the initial appeal, to the Fourth District Court of Appeal, to the point when they petitioned the California Supreme Court, their determination—and their team—had grown. The women knew the significance of what was being argued, and the gravity of any decision that would be rendered, from the moment this court agreed to hear their case.

The case had received national attention. The couple appeared twice on HBO's *Real Sports with Bryant Gumbel* and were featured on a multitude of other television and print media features. Lawyers from organizations including the ACLU, the National Center for Lesbian Rights, and the California Office of the Attorney General had filed "friend of the court" briefs in support of their case.

With B and Kendall on this momentous day was Kendall's mother, Truth; their original attorney, Lionel Price; and Jon Davidson, senior counsel for Lambda Legal. By the time the case reached the California Supreme Court, B and Kendall had been together as a couple for more than twelve years and domestic partners for six years. They lived together, filed their taxes together, owned property together, took turns taking out the trash, and did all of the other things most spouses do.

Coming from a proud German heritage, B achieved a high level of success in the male-dominated world of television advertising. Kendall describes B to others as a "duck" or an "iceberg" because of her ability to glide through situations with seeming ease, letting typical frustrations roll off her back while she internalized and compartmentalized any angst. This feature allows B to deal with almost any situation with a level head. An avid golfer, B used her comfort and prowess on the links to connect with her colleagues and clients. She is a people person who truly values her relationships.

Many of those relationships were tested during this experience. If nothing else, the seven-year ordeal exposed a new, more vulnerable side of B that allows her to embrace and share her feelings more openly today. Kendall, who has always known her partner to be driven and tenacious, feels that B's relentless pursuit for justice during this critical time was often the only thing that stood between them giving up the case and seeing it through.

Those who know Kendall would not hesitate to describe her as emotionally transparent. She has a knack for seeing the positive in many situations, yet will not hesitate to demonstrate her frustration or anger when warranted. She uses this straightforwardness to her advantage toward the right path. This case truly tested her.

Lionel Price was the couple's initial attorney. Up until this point in their lives, neither B nor Kendall had ever been involved in a legal squabble of any kind. Despite their professional careers, they were completely naive about the process—not knowing what to ask, expect, or demand from Lionel. As time passed, they became somewhat more sophisticated about how the legal process worked. That's when they reached out to Lambda Legal.

Lambda Legal is the largest and oldest legal organization committed to achieving full recognition of the civil rights of lesbians, gay men, bisexuals, transgender people, and those living with HIV through impactful litigation, education, and public policy. It is a nonprofit organization that does not charge for legal representation and receives no public funding. Jon Davidson was senior counsel for Lambda Legal at the time B and Kendall contacted them. Jon was interested in the case, and, after careful consideration of its merits and its alignment with Lambda's core mission, agreed to take the lead on the appeal process. B and Kendall immediately saw Jon as a smart, understated individual who was concerned with righteousness rather than personal accolades. He opened their eyes to their case's potential implications. Without Lambda's and Jon's involvement, B and Kendall are certain the case never would have gone any further.

At 9:00 a.m. on Thursday, May 26, 2005, seven justices—four women and three men in black robes—entered the courtroom of the California Supreme Court to begin hearing oral arguments. Oral arguments at this level are generally scheduled for an hour; thirty minutes per side. Jon Davidson initially argued for twenty-five minutes on B and Kendall's behalf. The opposing lawyer argued for the same amount of time, which was followed by a five-minute rebuttal from Jon. Because the justices asked a good deal of questions, the argument ran well over the allotted one-hour time frame.

Despite the TV-like grandeur of the proceedings, the day was a bit anticlimactic for B and Kendall—they knew the court's decision would not be made for some time. Yet the simple act of being able to be heard, truly heard, by seven representatives of the highest court in the state allowed them to exhale. They could take the case no further. They had battled their way as complete novices through a minefield of challenges to have their voices heard and to be given the opportunity to influence critical change.

B, Kendall, Jon, and Lionel walked out to the steps of the courthouse, where Jon answered questions from the media. They took a photograph to commemorate the day and then parted ways.

It would be a little over two months before they received the court's decision.

CHAPTER TWO

The Birthday Gift

1987

Close to twenty years before B and Kendall's appearance in the California Supreme Court courtroom, B was a media sales professional in San Diego, California, and a single woman with a passion for golf.

This particular spring day was filled with color: brilliant blue skies above a sparkling, emerald-green golf course, flower beds bursting with vibrant reds, yellows, and oranges. It was the kind of day that beckoned people to come out for fresh air and a round of golf. To be playing in the Kyocera Classic Pro-Am golf event with an LPGA pro was an exciting opportunity for B. This was the only LPGA event in San Diego and was hosted by Bernardo Heights Country Club (BHCC). Participating as an invited guest was one of the great perks of B's job as a television sales executive at CBS 8 San Diego. As she was enjoying this special day of golf with her clients, she imagined how awesome it would be to be a member of this great club. To play this course anytime she wished, rather than just once a year during an event, seemed too good to be true. She daydreamed about how incredible it would be to bring friends and clients here to share the wonderful golf she was experiencing that day.

After she and the rest of her foursome had finished their round, B decided to inquire about what it would take to become a member at BHCC. She figured it might be out of her league, but what the heck. She was loving her career in sales at CBS 8, and she was turning thirty-two. Wouldn't a golf membership be the perfect gift to give herself?

Much to B's surprise, she discovered membership was affordable. The club offered "Junior Executive" memberships, which would give her the option to pay the initiation fee over time. For the next few years, she would pay the yearly installment on her birthday and then, upon her thirty-fifth birthday, it would convert to a full family membership. Being a young professional with a decent golf game, B was welcomed by the board of directors with open arms. They wanted younger businessmen and women to entertain at the club, bring in clients to play golf, and host dinners and drinks afterward, which would help the club's profitability. It seemed to be a perfect fit for both B and the club, and she was thrilled with her purchase. It was truly a happy birthday!

B made friends easily at the club and over the years became one of its top women golfers. One year, when her game was at its best, she decided to join the Bernardo Heights women's golf team. It was intense, but as someone who had played competitive tennis in college, B loved being part of a team and challenging herself on the course. Given her low handicap, she was matched up to play in the number one spot and was partnered with the best player in the club, who had a two handicap. Although B felt intimidated, they turned out to be a ham-and-egg duo. Her golf partner always had B's back on the course. It was an amazing confidence builder for her game. They became both a hard to beat team and dear friends. It was a memorable time in B's life. They worked hard and played hard.

While on the team, B and her golf partner started playing a regular game with two other women. Since two of the foursome worked full time, they agreed to play on Saturdays. The standing Saturday tee time with this group was something B looked forward to all week. Unfortunately, Saturday was "men's day" at the club and women couldn't tee off until after 1:00 p.m. This was problematic because during shorter winter days, the group couldn't finish eighteen holes before it got dark.

B decided to challenge the board's decision to designate Saturday morning tee times solely for men. She petitioned the board to allow women to play on Saturday mornings, stressing that consideration should be given because, just like the men, many women in the club worked full time.

B was actually a bit shocked when the club ultimately saw her point and changed Saturday mornings to all-gender tee times. Although it took some time for her Saturday foursome to feel comfortable with a 9:00 a.m. tee time, they got used to it. The men's resentment over women on the course on Saturday mornings subsided after a few months as well. B's foursome played together for years, and B named the group "the Cronies."

When B became an equity member at BHCC, she was a young woman in the world of media sales. Having her own family membership to a prestigious country club not only satisfied her love of the game of golf, but it also leveled the playing field for her to entertain clients. Because the membership was considered an equity position, it meant B owned 1/320 of the land. Having a good time on the golf course was a natural, positive, and healthy way for her to gain trust and respect and to close business as a woman in a male-dominated industry—especially a woman who also happened to be gay.

CHAPTER THREE

Plus One

1993

Kendall and B met in 1993 through mutual friends. After developing a nice friendship, they started spending more time together. The more time they spent together, the more they enjoyed being together. Something between them just clicked. Neither had expected that. B found Kendall to be refreshing, open, and honest, with no hidden issues or drama. There was no facade. B had found her perfect match.

At first, Kendall thought B was out of her league. But as they got to know each other, Kendall found B to be warm, smart, articulate, and a really good listener. It soon became clear how much they had in common—both were hardworking and close with their families, and both loved to travel, entertain, and ski. Kendall remembers thinking, *This is the type of woman I would really like to be with.*

The women moved in together and began building a life as a couple in 1995. They filed taxes, co-owned property, were each other's beneficiaries and medical powers of attorney, and so on. They were as committed to each other as any two people could be without the legal recognition of a marriage. In 1999, when the domestic partnership law passed in California, they filed immediately—in fact, they were among the first fifty couples to register. At the time, it was the most formal relationship status recognized by the State of California for same-sex couples.

For years, B and Kendall were very much accepted at the club. They were among the youngest players there, which helped to provide a lighter energy in the clubhouse. Kendall, being a hobby mixologist, taught the bartenders how to make specialty martinis such as cosmopolitans and lemon drops. Everyone was friendly and welcomed the young group's vitality. It was clear to all that the two women were in a relationship and considered themselves a couple. The staff members at the club would argue over who got to serve them. Such a welcoming, engaging environment helped B and Kendall feel a bit closer to mainstream, something they both wanted and strived for. It was refreshing. They were comfortable at the club and felt at home. They were treated just like all the other members.

As Kendall's golf game started improving, their friends at the club wanted her to play more and perhaps fill in if one of the Cronies could not participate on Saturdays. Up to this point, Kendall had been playing as B's guest and was limited to six golf passes a year. At seventy dollars per round, on top of the hefty monthly dues B was already paying, it just didn't seem reasonable that Kendall needed to pay more according to the bylaws. This was unfortunate because the Cronies, as well as B's other friends, liked Kendall very much and encouraged her to be more a part of the golf experience. They had all become very social, going on ladies-only golf trips and meeting on Friday nights after golf for drinks and dinner—spouses included.

As it was well established that Kendall and B were a couple, and B was paying for a family membership, they felt it reasonable to ask the club to let Kendall play as B's spouse and enjoy all the same benefits the other spouses were afforded. After all, family membership not only offered privileges to a spouse, but, as an equity member, B was also a part owner in the club.

Sadly, despite B and Kendall's formal, state-recognized relationship status and B's family membership, the club refused to recognize them as a family. But the women considered themselves a family. They reasoned they should have the same rights and benefits as the Cronies and most other members who played with their spouses. Something had to change.

Naively—since, per her previous request, the board had agreed to change the rule and let women play on Saturday mornings—B thought it might be time to start working on either increased guest passes for Kendall or a significant-other policy. The two had an idea that they felt could work. There were twenty-one widows and widowers at the club who were in the same position as B and Kendall, other than the fact that they had the option to marry. B also had a bigger problem that complicated the issue: she was not totally out among her professional associations. She had intended to come out at CBS 8 San Diego, and it had backfired on her.

When B would attend work functions and go on the annual client incentive trip, a gay male friend of hers would always accompany her. She decided she no longer wanted to continue this charade she had created. It was time to be honest. So, at dinner one night with her former general sales manager, B explained to him how increasingly difficult it was to live two lives. She said she was planning to come out at work. Her former boss's reaction caught her off guard. He made it clear that he thought she would lose her job if she came out, and he very strongly urged her not to do it. He and B had always worked well together, and he knew the environment she was working under, so she trusted his belief that it was best for her career to not disclose her sexuality.

This was devastating to B. She loved her job and losing it was not an option. Therefore, concerning BHCC, teaming up with the widows and widowers seemed to be the only way she could move forward without outing herself in the process. It was never B and Kendall's intention to turn this into a gay rights issue. They only wanted to be able to play golf together, and how they did it didn't matter to them. Meeting with the widowed members in their position who also had family memberships was a good starting point. They reached out to each person and asked if they wanted to meet to discuss the options. Every one of them came to the meeting. B and Kendall felt extremely optimistic about the interest and 100 percent participation.

After many meetings, the group came up with a significant-other policy to present to the board. It would allow unmarried couples to assign a partner to their family membership. The crux of the issue for the widows and widowers was that if they remarried, they could lose their social security benefits—clearly not a viable option just to gain some additional golf benefits. Thus, they were eager to join this effort. This solution had the potential to also work out well for B and Kendall as being gay had nothing to do with the request, nor would they require any special consideration. Kendall would simply be B's significant-other member.

The club would benefit as well. Growing by twenty-two new members under this concept would be a substantial gain. In addition, the club's existing single members would be happy to share the cost of their membership with their significant others. And as they were always looking for new revenue streams, the club would benefit from the increase in food revenue, cart fees, locker fees, and other items that come with new members. It seemed to be a win-win for everyone.

The club did not see it that way. That's when all hell broke loose.

PERSONAL SPACE

LOVE

From Kendall: I met B a few years before we got together, but we weren't what you would call instant friends. The second time I saw her she didn't remember meeting me, and the third time, she remembered meeting me but couldn't remember my name. It was a bit of a bruise to my ego. As time went on and we saw each other at more gatherings, we became friendly acquaintances. When I finally got to spend some one-on-one time with her, I thought to myself, *Wow—what a great gal!* She was a total hottie! I quickly began to see the other side of B—her softer side. Never in a million years did I think we would end up together. Then when she learned I had just gone through a tough breakup, she called and asked me to dinner. I was surprised but, of course, I accepted the invitation on the spot. As the evening progressed, again, I learned more about B than I had known before. We had drinks at her house and she made me the worst drink I've ever had, some kind of peach nectar juice with vodka. It was awful, but I didn't care. I was just thrilled to be in her company. It became immediately clear that we actually had a lot in common—we were both hardworking, close to our families, and loved to travel, entertain, ski—and, of course, golf.

CHAPTER FOUR

Undesirables

1997

A few months later, B and Kendall received their answer from the club attorney, Tim Montrose. Tim was a member of BHCC, and, at the time, board secretary. Montrose had written to all 320 club members with a proposed change to the bylaws. In his written correspondence to the members, he made sure everyone was clear on the board's position: "The board does not recommend the proposal and voted 7:2 against passage." In his drafting of the proposal, he defined a *significant other* as someone who had shared a common residence with a member for at least a year. Only one significant other could be designated in any twelve-month period. In the event of the death of the member, membership assets could not be inherited. Then came one big hitch. After all of B and Kendall's efforts to get the single members to lobby for a significant-other policy, Montrose added a very specific criterion to the proposed bylaw change that the women clearly could not meet: the significant other "shall be of the opposite sex of the member."

At the September 1997 BHCC membership committee meeting, as expected, the proposed bylaw change was voted down. B, Kendall, and the widowed members were deflated. Monthly dues at Bernardo Heights were about $700, plus a food minimum, cart fees, and locker fees, no matter how many people were using a membership. For singles, the average monthly bill was between $750 and $1,000. B and Kendall felt their request was reasonable and mutually beneficial. Times were changing and clubs across San Diego were responding by adjusting for lifestyle differences and finding new revenue sources. The women personally called every private club in San Diego and found that most of them were working on the same kind of adjustments to help their single members that B and Kendall had proposed to BHCC.

They felt that BHCC had slammed the door in their faces. After the vote, one member consoled B by saying, “It’s generational. The older generation can’t understand this at all.” B believed that was true. At that time, the average age of a Bernardo Heights member was sixty-two years old—old enough to have compassion for the widows and widowers, as they could all find themselves in this situation sooner or later.

Kendall and B were perplexed and terribly disappointed. But they refused to give up. They tried again two years later when the group of single members, mostly widows, had grown to forty. They gathered the group together once again and came up with a new plan. This time, their proposal was to grant the right to designate a guest with whom the single member could play unlimited golf. Thinking the board might view that as too generous, they also proposed an alternative: that single members be given one guest pass per week. The long-range planning committee of the board reviewed their proposal and again rejected both options. Both sides were at an impasse.

The singles group was discouraged and soon disbanded. B and Kendall's efforts to work out a fair, reasonable solution had been rewarded with zero results. After three years, they hadn't gained any ground. They felt terrible for the widows, all of whom were older than they were by more than twenty years. Although their effort to help the group was behind them, the situation had become personal to B and Kendall. They felt they were being targeted, which infuriated them, and they were not going to let it go. They were determined to get to the bottom of it.

In 1999, the club hired a new general manager named Court Bolton. Coincidentally, Court's wife, Debra, owned a local company and B had handled Debra's company's television marketing campaign and consulted with her on all media concerns for almost ten years. Debra and B had also traveled together due to B's company offering an annual client incentive trip. On one trip, Debra had brought Court as her guest. B thought they made a lovely couple and was glad to see Debra so happy, since she had been a widow for some time.

One afternoon while B was on the driving range, Court approached her and asked why she had stopped holding the annual CBS 8 San Diego client golf event and the annual Make-A-Wish Foundation golf event at the club. The golf events alone brought in over ten thousand dollars. In the past, for each event, B would reserve the club on a Monday when it was normally closed and host about one hundred people for a light breakfast, golf, lunch, dinner, and an open bar. Court also asked B why she had stopped entertaining clients there.

"Court," said B, "I do not support a club that does not support me." She then told Court about her efforts with Kendall to improve single memberships over the previous four years. He was very surprised to hear about it, and he felt it was unfair as well.

"Let's go to the board and get this changed," he said.

Kendall and B were skeptical, given their history with the board. B had known Court for many years and Kendall had known him professionally as well. They trusted Court and knew he had an open mind. The following month, Court arranged a meeting with B, Kendall, and Craig Moulton, BHCC's president.

During the meeting, Craig gave Kendall and B the impression that he feared if the club made an exception for the women to be able to play as a family, it would open the floodgates to many other gay couples who would potentially want to join. The meeting ended abruptly with Court, B, and Kendall shaking their heads. They had their answer. Bernardo Heights was never going to be a club where gay couples would be allowed to join as a family.

Kendall and B decided it was time for them to meet with the entire board. They wrote the board a letter explaining their position. They felt very strongly that they deserved to play golf together on any given day, without being charged a guest fee for Kendall. They were not interested in redefining the club's couples events—weekend events that were held so husbands and wives could team up to play against other couples. B and Kendall did not wish to create any new controversy.

In the letter, they included the fact that they both worked full time and had thriving careers within the mainstream environment. Both of their jobs required high levels of professionalism, entertaining clients, and interaction with business and community leaders. Absurd as it seemed, they felt it necessary to assure the board that they knew how to conduct themselves in social situations and that their time spent at the club would be no exception.

The following month, the board held another meeting and Kendall and B were invited. A few of the board members did not know Kendall, so this meeting gave them the opportunity to meet her. Kendall introduced herself and shared her background and her passion for golf. As of this meeting, the couple had been together seven years.

B and Kendall shared with the board that they were among the first fifty couples to register for a domestic partnership within the State of California. They shared that they owned their home together as tenants in common and had a living trust that designated each other as beneficiaries. They had done everything available at the time to get as close as they could to being married. But according to the State of California, marriage was defined as a union between a man and a woman. That condition had kept Kendall from qualifying to golf under B's family membership—and Bernardo Heights had refused to work with them under any circumstances, citing the California State criteria.

The women shared that even though they were a different type of family, they considered themselves a family nonetheless. Since they both worked full time, Saturday and Sunday were the only days they could play together. This meant that a weekly guest pass for Kendall would work for them. They were very clear that this would be a cost-free solution for the club and would be enough to satisfy them. They made sure to express how greatly they would appreciate this consideration.

Looking back, B and Kendall feel sickened when they think about how much they pleaded and kowtowed to try to be accepted by board members who had offered nothing but hostility and discrimination. The fact that they had to go to such extremes was ridiculous and humiliating in equal measure.

They walked away from the meeting very hopeful. They had told the board their truth and had spoken from the heart. They had been kind, reasonable, patient, and respectful, especially so because most of the board members were their parents' ages. There was no hidden agenda—they just wanted to play golf together and were willing to settle for just one round a week. Fair and reasonable, right?

During the meeting, as in the previous meeting with Mr. Moulton, the board members hid behind the notion that providing any accommodation for B and Kendall would require a bylaw change, which would require a vote of the full membership. This the couple already knew. The previous board had voted 7:2 against supporting the measure—and without board support, the full membership vote would not have a chance to pass.

On January 2, 2001, B and Kendall received their answer from the board. They were advised to purchase a separate membership for Kendall so they could play golf together any time they wished, as well as enjoy all other membership privileges. The board also stated they could not amend the bylaws without a membership vote. The couple knew that 98 percent of club memberships were in the husband's name, meaning only men would be voting on the change. Without board support, the proposal would never pass.

Something even more infuriating: Although the board made it clear to B and Kendall that a full membership vote would be required for their proposal, the monthly Bernardo Heights newsletter revealed that the board had voted to change the "rules" not the bylaws to allow grandchildren of members to play unlimited free golf *without* conducting a full membership vote. So now hundreds of grandchildren had golf privileges while the request for a weekly guest pass for Kendall was simultaneously denied.

The message was finally crystal clear: *Gays not wanted.*

For a while, B and Kendall considered walking away from BHCC membership and joining another club, but they couldn't swallow that pill. They were deeply offended by the board's blatant ignorance and dismissal. B had been a member for more than twelve years. She and Kendall would not give the board the satisfaction of seeing them walk away.

Instead, they became even more determined. They knew they deserved consideration. They were not going to be dismissed by Bernardo Heights as undesirables. The grandchildren privileges had pushed them over the edge. The message from Bernardo Heights was received, but the club underestimated B and Kendall.

Quite frankly, B and Kendall underestimated themselves.

CHAPTER FIVE

Double Bogey

2001

Kendall and B shared their story about their treatment at the club at least a hundred times with colleagues and close friends. They felt times were changing. When they talked about their dilemma, the response was consistent: everyone was baffled that the club would not work with them on some sort of compromise.

One evening at a neighborhood gathering, their neighbor Martin, who was their attorney for estate planning, mentioned that he rented office space from an attorney named Lionel Price, who litigated these types of cases. He suggested B and Kendall give Lionel a call, if only to get his opinion and insight. So they did.

Being involved in a lawsuit is typically unpleasant—and at times can be completely debilitating. Most average citizens who have never sued anyone or been sued can't prepare themselves for it and may not have the capacity to understand the complexity and ugliness that comes with it. Most who have been through the experience wouldn't recommend it to anyone unless absolutely necessary. A lawsuit creeps into your every moment and waits for your attention. It's all-consuming.

After they realized they had taken the conversation with the club as far as they could on their own, Kendall and B hired Lionel Price as their attorney. They felt the need to separate themselves physically and emotionally from the process and rely on the advice of an expert dedicated to their issue. Lionel walked the couple through the basic process for making a claim against the club. He suggested the first step should be to draft a complaint against the club, but not actually file it. According to Lionel, this would signal to the club that they were serious—and if the board members were smart, they would take the time to sit down with them and work out some sort of accommodation.

As total novices, B and Kendall were admittedly a bit embarrassed about how little they knew or understood of the legal process. They tried to ask lots of questions but really did not know what to ask. Besides wanting to understand how they could come to some resolution and what the process would entail, they needed to know what it was going to cost them. At one point, Kendall asked Lionel point blank, "How much will this cost?"

Lionel responded, "It's like turning on a water faucet and having the handle break off in your hand with the water running."

In retrospect, Kendall and B knew they should have sought opinions and feedback from more than one attorney. But Lionel presented himself as the fatherly, supportive figure they felt they needed. They embarked on the process of bringing him up to speed on what had happened and laying out their case for equal treatment. They were still optimistic that an amicable and non-litigious understanding could be achieved.

In B and Kendall's opinion, the club had made several mistakes. First, they seemed to be locked in on their position—*we're not going to let these two gay women tell us what to do*—and they were going to fight tooth and nail. No negotiation, no accommodation. *See you both in court.* Since the women were both successful sales professionals, they knew the importance of understanding the other side. What was the other side's perspective on the situation? They knew that was how the best negotiations happen, and it was how they still hoped to resolve this issue.

The second mistake was the club's reckless ignorance in their communication to B and Kendall and to the membership. Additionally, and even more damaging, was their wink-and-nod policy for single heterosexual male members *that continued during the lawsuit.* And yet, the club was a private entity whose bylaws specifically and intentionally excluded the simple request B and Kendall were making. That's what empowered the couple to keep going even when they suffered serious setbacks. That's what kept them fired up to continue pressing forward.

PERSONAL SPACE

GROWING UP KENDALL

My parents married in the early '60s and a couple of years later had my brother and me. They bought a beautiful home in Covina, California. When I was a year old, they moved to a rented house in Newport Beach, and we never again lived in a house we owned. A few years later, we moved to a duplex that was across the street from the beach but had to move again after just nine months. This time, our family had become close with another family that was planning a move to Laguna Beach. Because it had better schools, we moved there—so I grew up in Laguna Beach. I know this makes a certain image come to mind, but that wasn't our experience. We were truly middle class. My parents barely scraped by to stay there because it had a great community and schools. Although this was a town where almost nobody rented, I lived in eight different rented houses between kindergarten and graduation from Laguna Beach High School. Most of the time we only had one car—usually an old beater that my dad used for work. I remember one car where the reverse gear didn't work and at times, we all had to get together and push the car out of its parking spot. I also remember my mom putting a check in an envelope and taping it to the door when a man was coming to the house to turn off our electricity. We lived in

Laguna Beach, such a glorious place, and yet we had no money most of the time.

I'm so grateful for the sacrifices my parents made to keep us in Laguna. I couldn't have had a better childhood. I spent summers at the beach, doing fun things that didn't cost a dime—hanging out with my buddies, boogie boarding, playing paddle board, jumping off the rocks, or swimming through the blowhole. We had so much freedom to just be kids. When I go to my reunions, I see friends I've known since kindergarten. Laguna was magical at the time, and I feel so fortunate to have grown up there.

CHAPTER SIX

Out of Bounds

2001

The more B and Kendall shared their frustrations about Kendall not being permitted to play golf under B's membership, the more they started hearing stories from other members and friends about the club's double standards regarding special privileges. One of the Cronies told B that she had played with her then-boyfriend, a member, for over a year, until they eventually married. With a mere wink that meant "this is my spouse," they enjoyed unlimited free golf.

Another one of B's dear friends, Connor Jeffers, admitted to her that he was not married to his live-in girlfriend, whom he considered his spouse. And they were allowed to play as a family. Furious that B and Kendall were being ostracized, Connor went to address the issue with Court Bolton, the club's general manager. Court told him to just play along, that there were other members also playing as married who were not. Kendall and B were unaware of this situation. Court stated to Connor: "We will work it out with you and your family after this lawsuit is behind us."

A few months later, Connor walked away from his membership in protest and joined another club. B and Kendall will always be grateful for his support and integrity. They remain friends to this day. He ultimately signed a sworn declaration to the facts above and spoke openly about the situation during media interviews. It was friends like Connor who gave the women the confidence to keep fighting.

Once it was clear the club wasn't interested in working with them, the couple filed a lawsuit against BHCC in May 2001—the draft complaint that they had presented to the club—in the hope that, once they showed their cards, the club may want to work something out. After all, they had spent well over a year trying to reach an amicable solution. But the club refused to negotiate and drew a ridiculously hard line. The club sent a letter to all the members that stated:

> *We are writing this letter for the purpose of providing you with an update on the litigation that we advised you on May 16, 2001, had been filed against BHCC. B. Birgit Koebke, one of our regular members and her domestic partner, Kendall E. French, who is not a member, filed a lawsuit on May 11, 2001, in the Superior Court of San Diego County. The basis for their claim is that they are not provided with the same membership and guest privileges accorded legally married members and, therefore, are discriminated against on the basis of their gender and/or sexual preference. These assertions are simply false. Ms. Koebke has never been denied the privileges of Regular membership, as provided for in the Bylaws, Rules and Regulations of BHCC.*

> *In support of their claims, Ms. Koebke and Ms. French allege that more than thirty-five club members, specifically identified by name in their Second Amended Complaint, are either not married or improperly hold title to their membership. We are looking into these claims.*
>
> *The Board of Directors determined it was in the long-term best interests of BHCC to contest these meritless charges and, in so doing, preserve for the membership the right to determine for ourselves how and under what circumstances membership and guest privileges should be defined.*
>
> *There is a Case Management Conference scheduled before the Court in January 2022, at which time the Court will assign a trial date and set various other deadlines. Thereafter, our attorneys intend to file a motion to dismiss the entire action.*

BHCC board secretary Tim Montrose's law firm represented the club, which, to B and Kendall, appeared to be a significant conflict of interest. As both a club member and the club's board secretary, he was not remotely impartial, and his law firm would most certainly benefit from a prolonged dispute. Yet, the members didn't protest and must not have cared about getting objective legal advice. The club was now being advised by one of its own members, who did not recuse himself in advising the club on what was best for it legally, versus the club's personal views on same-sex couples. It's not hard to see his bias in his correspondence to club members.

As an example, in one letter, Montrose wrote:

> *"If the club is ruled in Ms. Koebke's and Ms. French's favor, the club would have to accept the extension of club privileges to significant others whether they be male/female, female/female, or male/male. In other words, the court would have to find that the California legislature's strong public policy of favoring marriage should be ignored." He continued, "The BHCC Board of Directors, past and present, have always attempted to follow the bylaws. The Board of Directors recognizes the state of California's strong public policy favoring marriage and believes that BHCC supports that policy as a family-oriented organization."*

Montrose and BHCC hired Morrison & Foerster, one of the biggest legal firms in Los Angeles, to assist in their defense. The choice was interesting and caused quite a stir within that firm. The lead attorney, John Shiner, had represented the Jonathan Club in Los Angeles, defending discriminatory practices against women and minorities. That case went all the way to the California Supreme Court, and Shiner lost.

Also, Morrison & Foerster had a track record of fighting for gay rights, so it was rumored that many of their attorneys within the firm were not happy with John Shiner for taking on the BHCC case, which sought to protect a private club's efforts to limit gay rights. It seemed clear that the club was trying to create an uncomfortable atmosphere for B, perhaps hoping she would resign. One day B, apparently by accident, received her monthly membership bill with a line-item charge for "Legal bills surcharge for B. Koebke lawsuit." It appeared that all of the members were being assessed a monthly charge on their bill, ranging from twenty dollars to around seventy dollars, to cover legal fees for the "Koebke suit." Now the couple knew why so much hatred was being directed toward them by other members. Interestingly, it was rumored that the club's legal fees were actually covered by its business liability insurance—so what was the monthly assessment all about?

Clients B would bring to the club began to admit they felt uncomfortable. When a client B was hosting approached one of her old friends in the clubhouse and was treated rudely, that was the last time she entertained a client there.

Each visit to the club became less tolerable for B and Kendall. When they arrived at the driving range, members on both sides of them would abruptly leave. When they played golf together and asked to join a twosome, they would be rebuffed. When they sat in the bar, people would get up and move to another table. One member was so belligerent that when they sat down for dinner one night, he stood up at his table and demanded to be moved "as far away from these two as possible. Right now." His voice was so loud it could be heard across the restaurant. The staff was mortified and disgusted by this behavior. It caused such a disturbance, the next day the new general manager, Stanley, called B and Kendall at home and apologized.

The women began to limit their time in the clubhouse. The membership B had once been so proud to purchase, the place they did business and engaged with friends, the course they called their second home, and the game over which Kendall and B bonded and grew even closer were all spoiled. The couple felt purposefully ostracized and alienated.

How innocent B and Kendall were to think both parties could be mutually respectful and work things out accordingly. This wasn't about money or services. It wasn't about family or fairness. It was about the women not fitting the image of what a small group of people felt was right. As long as they kept their heads down and did not ask to be acknowledged as a couple, all was well. B's membership fees were accepted and no questions were asked. But the moment they asked to be treated equally and recognized as a family, the pleasantries evaporated. They never lost their cool. They bit their tongues and were as gracious and patient as possible. After all, they had served the club a draft lawsuit that hadn't been filed, signaling their willingness to come to a compromise. They still didn't understand how they became the bad guys who had somehow wronged the club.

As time went on, the situation at the club turned into what felt like high school drama. Any association with Kendall and B resulted in members being shunned by other members. The Cronies group they had played and socialized with since B first got her membership walked away from them due to social pressure. As new members joined the club, current members would pull them aside, point to the couple, and tell them to stay away if they wanted to be accepted. When B went to the sign-up sheet in the women's locker room to sign up to play on a team, like she had done three years in a row, no one else joined. After two weeks, someone crossed out B's name and, miraculously, others joined overnight. B and Kendall got the message. These country club women, unfortunately, had succumbed to peer pressure.

Julie Stillwell, a member of the LPGA and a golf professional, soon joined the club. She submitted a declaration stating that there was hostility toward Kendall and B at BHCC.

She stated after she golfed with B that members told her she would not have a single friend at BHCC if she continued playing with B and Kendall. She also documented hearing a comment by a club member who crudely suggested that the couple put on a skit on the putting green demonstrating how they have sex and charge admission to help pay for the lawsuit. And she confirmed that BHCC did not require members to register their guests, as they had claimed, but that Kendall and B had to sign a registration book every time they played together.

The whole club had turned against them, and it was hell. Even one of B's favorite golfing buddies, Luke, turned away. For years, Luke and B would golf together in the late afternoon after work because his wife did not play. When B first told Luke she was gay, he sent a dozen roses to her office with a lovely note to express his acceptance and appreciation for her honesty. A few years later, during a dinner conversation with Luke and his wife at Kendall and B's house, Kendall innocently mentioned the story of Luke sending roses to B. His wife, who hadn't heard about it, became furious and did not speak to him for a week.

B had often complained to Luke about her dilemma with the club, and he always listened and shared his personal challenges with her as well. He told her he considered her his best friend outside of his marriage. B had a lot of respect for Luke, and they enjoyed their time together. He was a good and generous friend to B and Kendall; he would fly them in his jet to Vegas for dinner and to Deer Valley to ski. B believed they had an honest, open relationship.

After B served the club with the lawsuit, she was surprised to find out that years earlier Luke had listed a friend's son as his own son. He had been playing at the club all that time with full privileges. Luke always advised B, "Don't rock the boat at the club. Leave things alone; everyone likes you." When she found out his faux son had played golf at the club for free for years, she was appalled at the hypocrisy. That revelation ended the friendship, and Luke later turned a large group of men against B and Kendall. Perhaps he felt he needed to hurt B back, as if the hurt was not bad enough already.

Another open-minded couple went out on a limb to try to recruit others to support B and Kendall. This failed—it received no backing from anyone. The wife called B in tears, saying she and her husband had received threats from other members. Their hearts had been in the right place to try to help, but they eventually disassociated themselves from the women as well. B and Kendall understood—this wasn't their friends' fight. They were at the club to play golf and have fun. Life is difficult enough—who wants this hassle?

The main purpose of joining a country club, in addition to playing golf, is gaining a built-in social life. Friendships develop quickly in this environment. Or so they thought. B and Kendall were alone now. If they wanted to play, they played together as a twosome or B played solo. Around this time, B made a cold call to the Lambda Legal Defense and Education Fund at the suggestion of a friend. Lambda Legal is the nation's oldest and largest nonprofit advocacy group for the civil rights of gay women and men. To B's surprise, in the era of voicemail and auto attendants, the senior counsel for Lambda Legal, Jon Davidson, answered his own phone. He had a kind voice. He and B hit it off immediately, and she shared the facts of their case with him. Although he was receptive and gracious with his time, he was not in a position to get involved because the women were still being represented by Lionel Price at the trial court level. Jon encouraged them to keep him updated on the progress of the case. B later learned that Jon was considered to be one of the most respected attorneys in the country—and that Jon's answering the phone would turn out to be the luckiest moment of B and Kendall's legal journey.

As often happens in legal proceedings, months passed as multiple complaints and amendments caused delay after delay. So while the lawsuit was at an impasse, B decided she would make a last-ditch effort and attend one more general membership meeting. She and Kendall still believed the entire membership needed to hear why they had served the club with the lawsuit. They wanted the members to know that, under Tim Montrose's direction, the board gave them no alternative but to hire an attorney. They had tried to find a compromise for years to handle their situation in an amicable manner. Maybe they could still solve this among the membership and not need to engage in legal proceedings.

B attended the meeting even though she was not considered a member in good standing. Kendall was not a member, and B received a phone call the night before warning that if Kendall tried to attend, she would be turned away at the door. The meeting was held at the new auditorium at a local high school, which was large enough to hold the now-640 members and spouses. When B entered, she could see the seas part. B's last remaining friend and ally, Bob Gold, sat staunchly beside her, offering his support.

When the facilitator raised the subject of the lawsuit, B bravely stood and introduced herself to the entire membership.

Her hands were sweating, her stomach burning. Time seemed to have stopped for her at this moment. She spoke from the heart:

> *Good evening, everyone. I am B Koebke, and I am really sorry I had to serve the club with a lawsuit. Your board, under Tim Montrose's guidance, gave us no alternative. I am here today to ask for your compassion and support. For years, I have tried to work this out with your board to no avail. Some of you must know someone who is gay—a son, a daughter, or a friend. If you don't know, Kendall and I are gay. We cannot legally get married and join the club as a couple. We have a domestic partnership filed with the State of California and we own our home together. We will settle for weekly golf guest passes for Kendall to put an end to this. We just want to play golf together. We do not wish to cause any distress; we would have never entered into a lawsuit as we dislike any attorney involvement. Please find it in your heart to do the right thing. Let us work this out among us, as we all own this club together. Please reconsider, before we go down a path neither side wants. Thank you so much for listening.*

B sat down, numb, trembling. She had finally said to the entire membership what she needed to say. She had pleaded. She was hoping for some compassion, some understanding, and perhaps some changing of minds. She was wrong. Again.

Two people clapped; everyone else was silent. Stone-cold silent. You could hear a pin drop in the large auditorium. What was wrong with these people? During the longest silence of B's life, Bob squeezed her hand. Here she was, a forty-year-old woman, asking for acceptance and consideration, and all but two members shunned her.

That was the final turning point. B knew she and Kendall had explored every option and had given it their all to handle things reasonably. It was now out of their hands. She was exhausted. With tears in her eyes, she drove home in the slow lane feeling numb and deflated—but not defeated.

CHAPTER SEVEN

Depositions

2001–2002

More than a decade later, as B sits at her desk in her kitchen in San Diego, she reflects on all the depositions from the BHCC lawsuit during the years of 2001 and 2002. Sunshine pours through the back windows, filling the room with welcome natural light and warmth. Beyond the patio and canyon hillside lie the rolling greens, forgiving fairways, and plush rough of the game she and Kendall love. Even in the worst of times, golf has been an escape.

With an apprehensive heart, she goes to the attic and stares at the twenty-two legal-size boxes from their lawsuit, tucked away in the very back, resting on dusty boards. She suddenly experiences a wide range of raw emotions, not the least of which is rage. The lawsuit is now in the past, but the emotional gash will never fully heal. Four boxes alone contain copies of depositions, many of them from former so-called friends. B was always confident and proud of the stance she took, so being deposed, though violating by nature, never got to her. But the toll of having to witness former friends being deposed against her and Kendall truly tested her faith in people.

For two full days in November 2001, B was deposed by the club's law firm, Morrison & Foerster, at their offices in San Diego. Kendall and B arrived together, on time, but their attorney, Lionel Price, showed up late. Lionel's tardiness did not sit well with them, but they had never been deposed before—they wondered if it was lawyerly posturing.

Also attending the spectacle was a videographer, a certified shorthand reporter, and an entourage of others including three additional attorneys from Morrison & Foerster, BHCC's attorney, Tim Montrose, and club board president Craig Moulton. It seemed their primary intent was to intimidate B and Kendall. The women had watched enough television dramas to know that this felt more like a murder case than a suit over golf privileges. In retrospect, it should have been a sign to them of the potential significance of this case.

After the late start of the deposition, it seemed the first two hours were spent arguing among the attorneys over what time and how long they would break for lunch. It was a fiasco.. They could not believe this three-ring circus marked the start of their proceedings.

For two days, the attorneys jockeyed for position. The end result of this posturing was B's deposition, which was a document of five hundred pages—as long as a novel. It took everything in her power to remain calm and answer the attorneys' ridiculous questions again and again. They went out of their way to try to throw her and make her as uncomfortable as possible. At one point, Mr. Shiner asked, "What does *sexual preference* mean to you?" Followed by, "Do you have a sexual preference?" Such questions implied that one day B might prefer a woman while the next day she might prefer a man.

And what did this have to do with denying her and Kendall the right to be recognized as a couple? Would they ask this of a heterosexual couple? As time dragged on, Mr. Shiner's questions became increasingly ludicrous and insulting.

B and Kendall sacrificed two precious vacation days for this farce with an end result of countless billable hours. They couldn't help but notice the clear motivation of some attorneys to create unnecessary, drawn-out disagreements would appear for the sake of their billable hours. The money spent by BHCC in attorney fees alone must have been exponentially more than a membership fee. And for what?

At the end of the two-day ordeal, Kendall and B felt embarrassed for the attorneys and disgusted by the process. They were ashamed that they had been forced to engage in such discourse when surely, as grown adults, they could have worked things out in a respectful and uncomplicated manner. To them, this seemed to be a preposterous way to make a living. And they were sickened at the money that this was costing. Into what rabbit hole had they fallen? The couple would sit at home on Friday nights—their regular date night—contemplating how they got into this situation. They questioned themselves about what they could have done to avoid this lawsuit. There was nothing glamorous about this process. It was all-consuming.

More depositions loomed. Lionel Price insisted that *all* of Kendall and B's former friends and *all* of the board members at the club be deposed to uncover whether or not they were given special membership consideration that was not granted to the women. B and Kendall questioned this strategy. They wanted him to hear their thoughts about who he should speak to and the questions he should ask. But Lionel was adamant, so they agreed. After all, he was the one with legal experience, and they needed to trust that he knew best.

B and Kendall sat in on every deposition, spending vacation time, lunchtime, and evenings after work. They were reasonably sure that the club had coached the deponents to give canned answers such as: "I don't recall," "I'm not sure," or "I don't know," as these phrases were universally used by every person. After B's two-day ordeal, she and Kendall insisted that the depositions not be videotaped. It was an unnecessary expense. They sat in on the depositions because they wanted to see what Lionel was asking, what people were saying, and how their money was being spent.

Most of the depositions were held at the club in one of the smaller conference rooms. They were attended by Lionel, a shorthand stenographer, B, and five to seven people from Morrison & Foerster and Bernardo Heights. Kendall and B felt that deposing them seemed like a total waste of the club's money since nothing new had been discovered, and the depositions basically confirmed what Kendall and B had presented to the club from the beginning. B's "friend" Luke—the member with the phony son—avoided being served his subpoena a total of five times. Unfortunately, hundreds of their dollars were spent to have the individual trying to serve him camp out in front of his house to catch him. It was clear that this was a game to Luke, and he went to great lengths to avoid being served. He obviously had a lot to hide.

The most significant ammunition Kendall and B had was the signed declaration of Connor Jeffers. It documented his conversation with the general manager, Mr. Bolton, who had said there were other members playing as married who were not. It was established that Kendall and B were the only ones who were required to sign a guest book. It also became irrefutable that every member could list any spouse's name or any child as their own without having to produce proof.

The depositions proved that the club's rules were treated as a free-for-all based largely on the honor system, and that the club chose to enforce the rules arbitrarily at best, and selectively and punitively at worst. Most of the members who were deposed agreed the club had singled out Kendall and B and turned against them. It was clear that the club easily could have made the decision to accommodate them. What the depositions did not reveal was why that decision was not made.

PERSONAL SPACE

GROWING UP B

I had a very adventurous childhood and very adventurous parents. We are all first-generation German and lived in a very sweet little town of Bremen, Germany. I was not ready at four years old for the German kindergarten. By the time I got to first grade, I already had been identified as a slow learner and sat at the back of the class. No one figured out that I needed glasses and was dyslexic. My mom worked patiently to help me with reading, writing, tying my shoes, and telling time. All those things were extremely difficult for me.

Two years later, my dad got a job in Santiago, Chile. I loved my school in Santiago with half the day taught in Spanish and the rest of the day in German. I thrived, outgrew my disabilities, and gained the confidence I needed to do well in school. After two years, we had to return to Germany, but within two months, my father was offered a job in Los Angeles. Three languages in twelve years was a lot, but it gave me a strong foundation to build on.

Coming to the US was a wonderful opportunity for all of us, but money was tight, so we all worked and contributed. I was amazed to see all the swimming pools in people's backyards. Many Americans had dogs and cats and enough space for them to roam around in. The kitchens had big refrigerators and freezers, and there were huge supermarkets with everything one could want. Complete strangers said hi as they passed in the streets—Americans were so friendly! Best of all, California had sunshine all year long. My family rented a small apartment for a year until we found a house we could afford. It was nothing special but it had a swimming pool—that was all I saw! Wow! I was in heaven. The American dream came true for us. I even got a cat. Life was wonderful.

CHAPTER EIGHT

The Raw Deal

2002

On June 28, 2002, B and Kendall received their answers. They had witnessed what seemed to be revealing and damning depositions of people associated with BHCC. They had filed multiple amended complaints. After all that, even when it seemed obvious that BHCC had been caught red-handed, rather than compromise with the couple, the club filed a motion for summary judgment. In simple terms, this filing asked the court to make a ruling on the merits of the case based on the facts before it without going to trial.

San Diego Superior Court Judge Charles R. Hayes ruled in favor of BHCC, granting their motion for summary judgment, effectively throwing out B and Kendall's entire case. He cited that the club "did not provide different privileges for the plaintiffs than to the other unmarried couples." In an interview with *Golf for Women*, John Shiner, the attorney from Morrison & Foerster representing BHCC, said: "The club, in this situation, did not treat people differently based on gender or sexual preference. And the court found there was no evidence that they did."

B was working out on her exercise bike when she heard the news. She was shocked. She stopped pedaling and sat on the bike for a long time. Kendall walked in the door soon after. She was so angry she could hardly speak. What went wrong? How did they fail? What could they have done differently? They had wasted their time and money and had compromised their friendships and their spirit. They still strongly believed they deserved their day in court.

The following week, then-president of BHCC, Walt Chambers, sent a letter to the members announcing that the lawsuit had been dismissed. He stated: *"While the Plaintiffs do have the opportunity to appeal, we hope that they realize the futility of such an attempt and allow the club to exist as bylaws dictate and the will and the spirit of the membership demanded."*

Once again, the club's treatment of B and Kendall, citing "the will and the spirit of the membership demanded" disgusted them. They were worthy of membership too.

Initially, Kendall and B's fight had been about playing golf together as a family. Period. For a while, that was their simple focus. They finally accepted the fact that it always had been about something else for the club. As long as they didn't ask for equal treatment, they were befriended and included. But the moment they stepped out of their lane, everything changed. With this decision, the message was loud and clear. Every member of the club had a vote, and virtually none of them had used it to do the right thing. For that, they should be ashamed.

The couple felt as if they had lost their faith in humanity. Had they been so blind they could see only good in everyone? Sadly, this was a sign of the times. The members believed they were right as much as B and Kendall did. They had been naive to think people would come around with time.

For the next few weeks, B and Kendall were in a fog. They worked mindlessly and moped around the house, still in shock that the club got away with dismissing them. They had numerous difficult discussions about what to do next. Should they walk away and move on with their lives? Or buckle up and fight on to prove what they knew to be true—that BHCC had a wink-and-nod policy for straight members in violation of their own bylaws? Members were sneaking fake spouses and children onto the course under their memberships, while the club was sticking to its guns when it came to not recognizing the legitimate familial relationship between Kendall and B.

The women knew that the club was discriminating against them, which continued to gnaw at them. To date, they had spent over $45,000 and had nothing to show for it. That scenario felt so wrong on so many levels. They knew it would take them years to pay everything off. To make the situation even more challenging and frightening, there was a rumor that the club would be coming after the couple for their legal fees because the case had been dismissed on the basis that the club considered the lawsuit frivolous.

People who knew the women knew they would never throw in the towel and would ultimately figure out how to move forward. They never ran away when the going got tough. But could they afford to spend the kind of money it would take to move forward with an appeal? For the first time, B and Kendall were panicked.

CHAPTER NINE

Cold Call

2002

B and Kendall had continued to send Jon Davidson all the developments in their case during those turbulent years in the trial court. It was only after the case was dismissed and they had exhausted most of their resources that they once again formally approached Lambda Legal for help. Despite the nature of the case and its alignment with Lambda's mission statement, the firm expressed some hesitancy in getting involved. Jon was transparent about these considerations. On the upside, Jon told B and Kendall that they were smart, articulate, assertive, and passionate. He empathized with them about the indignity of suddenly being looked down upon simply for who they loved when all they asked was to be treated like everyone else. From a legal perspective, he told them he felt they had a good argument since they had conducted themselves the same as would any married couple. In addition to living together, co-owning property, being each other's beneficiaries, etc., they had also executed a private domestic partnership agreement well before the

State of California formally recognized such a document as legally binding. And personally, he respected how much this meant to the couple.

The concern about taking on the case came from a different perspective. Comparatively speaking, B and Kendall were privileged. And, on the surface, this was about the right to play golf together. For an organization like Lambda—which relies on donations for its funding and has a limit on the number of cases they can pursue each year—the optics and impact of its litigation are important considerations. The women's reasoning was that their privilege was what enabled them to bring their case this far—they were able to do it because they could afford it. Jon knew, although their ability to play golf together as a family may have been the impetus, their case was about so much more. It's true that Jon and Lambda could take on cases for less privileged people who suffered from far more onerous and critical discrimination. But a positive outcome in this case could set an incredibly important and impactful precedent as gay marriage and gay rights were being debated across the country.

In convincing the legal department at Lambda to take this case, Jon urged them to remember the strategy of the late, great Ruth Bader Ginsberg. When she was head of the ACLU Women's Rights Project, she would frequently take on sex discrimination cases where the victims of the discrimination were men. Given that many jurors and judges were men, she believed these cases would resonate better with her audience. She was right. She was able to establish great precedent for discrimination cases against women by using cases that involved men as the victims of discrimination. Jon made a similar argument to the Lambda legal department. Lots of judges belonged to, or were familiar with, country clubs. This case had a very good chance of resonating with them. Jon convinced Lambda's legal department to allow him to pursue the case through the appellate courts. The couple thereafter referred to him as their "knight in shining armor."

Not long after B and Kendall's case was thrown out of the trial court, B received a call at work from a reporter named Marcia Chambers. Chambers was an award-winning editor at *Golf Digest* magazine and *Golf for Women*. Ms. Chambers's specialty was writing about discrimination in private clubs. A fellow at Yale Law School's program for journalists, she had written for *The New York Times* and the *National Law Journal*. Of course, B made time for her.

During their conversation, Marcia said she would like to interview B and Kendall for an article in *Golf for Women*. However, before Marcia made the trip to San Diego, she reached out to her cousin, an attorney who also lived in San Diego. Marcia asked him to look at the dismissal of B and Kendall's case so he could share his thoughts and insights regarding their lawsuit. Marcia asked his opinion as to whether they had received a raw deal with the dismissal of the case by Judge Hayes. Her cousin felt that they had, which was consistent with rumors on the street. Kendall and B later discovered that Marcia had done a great deal of her own research on their case before she contacted them.

When Marcia learned that Jon Davidson was now handling the case, she was even more intrigued. She was also becoming increasingly enthusiastic about writing an article about the couple. Marcia had interviewed Jon when he was a top litigator with the ACLU and had also consulted with him for her 1995 book *The Unplayable Lie*. Jon had won a major discrimination case that same year against the Peninsula Golf & Country Club near San Francisco. That case marked a landmark ruling by the California Supreme Court. In his argument, Jon had said that golf and country clubs in general would now have to meet the narrow definition of what constitutes a truly private and social club.

In that case, Jon relied on the Unruh Civil Rights Act, adopted by the State of California in 1959. It stated: “All persons within the jurisdiction of this state are free and equal, and no matter what their sex, race, color, religion, ancestry, national origin, disability, medical condition, genetic information, marital status, sexual orientation, citizenship, primary language, or immigration status are entitled to the full and equal accommodations, advantages, facilities, privileges, or services in all business establishments of every kind whatsoever.”

In her January 2003 *Golf for Women* article, Marcia Chambers wrote about Mr. Davidson’s successful arguments in the 1995 case: “In a landmark ruling, the California Supreme Court agreed with Davidson that the Unruh Act applied to Peninsula Country Club. Davidson had argued that the Unruh Act, which bars discrimination in all business establishments of every kind, applied to Peninsula CC because the club was available for business purposes.” Further, in his interview with Marcia, Davidson said that in many ways, Bernardo Heights had more public attributes than Peninsula CC—even advertising its availability to the public for social events on its website. “The club chose a gate by which to keep Koebke and French out,” he said. “The gate they chose is the one thing that people in same-sex relationships can't access: marriage. Someone who is heterosexual can get married if he or she wants the benefits. But clearly, marriage is not available to people in same-sex relationships."

The interview by Marcia Chambers was the catalyst for a string of positive media coverage that B and Kendall had only dreamed about. Most of the participants in the interviews were supportive of their side. The women were thrilled to finally receive some positive encouragement. It was a game changer—up to this point, they were accustomed to being perceived as the bad guys. Now they had Lambda Legal, Marcia Chambers, and national media support. Kendall and B could not believe their good fortune. Their Friday night date nights became a whole lot more enjoyable.

In October 2003, Lambda Legal filed an appeal to overturn the decision by Judge Hayes on behalf of Koebke and French. The appeal would decide whether a business can give benefits to persons who are married and can deny those same benefits to persons who cannot get married. If Lambda Legal won, and the summary judgment was overturned, the Koebke and French case would go to trial. B and Kendall had high hopes. They finally had the most important weapon they needed: a team of remarkable lawyers, which finally leveled the playing field. The reach and depth of their case became much stronger with Lambda's involvement. This was no longer just about B and Kendall. And it wasn't just about golf. A victory would have a far-reaching positive impact for all gay people in the state of California.

Once the appeal was filed, the couple rarely went to the club. The treatment toward them had been dreadful before the appeal, so they could only imagine how bad it would be now. However, they did continue paying their monthly dues to Bernardo Heights in order to have standing in the case. If they stopped paying now because they were not using the club, the case would be moot. There was too much at stake. They paid to play at other golf courses instead, knowing that the fees paid to Bernardo Heights were a necessary means to a just end.

PERSONAL SPACE

COLLEGE AND CAREER—KENDALL

Growing up, I was more social than an academic. I just squeaked by in school. My mom placed a lot of value on education, and going to college was nonnegotiable. Even though there was no money for college, I applied and got accepted to Oregon and Chico State. I went to Santa Barbara City College and then Orange Coast College—junior colleges were free back then. When I was ready to transfer to a university, my grandfather called my mom and out of the blue offered to pay for my last two years of college. I transferred to San Diego State University and graduated with a degree in public administration.

While at San Diego State, I took a business English class where we had to research a career that interested us. My mom had just met a woman who worked for Disneyland Hotel as a catering manager responsible for weddings and special events. By the end of the research paper, I knew I wanted to be in the hotel business, and I wanted to work for Marriott. In 1983, they were an up-and-coming hotel chain that had a management training program. Unlike other big hotel chains I interviewed for my paper, Marriott was encouraging. They said there was no specific timeline or special requirements—my success depended on me, my work ethic, and my eagerness. As a person who isn't afraid to work hard and be focused, I liked the idea of a company where I could create my own destiny.

The plan was in place: get my foot in the door at the first Marriott in San Diego, which was about to open, and work my way into the management training program.

I applied as soon as the hotel opened even though the only position available was banquet server. My instincts were right. Marriott had a lot of opportunities, and I could move up based on my hard work and focus. In about a year, almost to the day, I was in the management training program. Upon completing the program, I was offered a sales position at the Marriott hotel and was in the hotel business for fifteen years. I made a couple of shifts into different industries before moving into pharmaceutical sales with GlaxoSmithKline Pharmaceuticals, where I stayed until I retired fourteen years later as a District Sales Manager.

CHAPTER TEN

Nits in the Wind

2003

With Lambda Legal on their side, B and Kendall had a whole new surge of energy, enthusiasm, and vigor for their case. Five years earlier, they never could have imagined that the biggest gay rights group in America would join forces with them. Lambda had a full team of lawyers across the country, with offices in many major cities. They had the experience, resources, and a genuine vested interest instead of billable hours. B and Kendall couldn't have predicted that pursuing the right to have golf privileges for Kendall as a part of B's family membership would turn into a national case about marriage rights. What an improbable change of events. Neither woman had foreseen the magnitude of this case.

In her *Golf for Women* article, Marcia Chambers called B and Kendall "the outsiders." Now they had become, as Jon Davidson called them, "the accidental activists." This was not their intention, but thanks to the discrimination from BHCC, that was who they became.

Time and patience made all the difference in the world. B and Kendall's persistence and personal involvement in the case were the key to moving forward, regardless of obstacles. Their initial understanding was that once someone turned their case over to an attorney, that would be the end of their worry and stress. How wrong that was. At this transformation point, their participation was encouraged and had become crucial. Surprisingly, their own ignorance and naivete worked to their advantage and, in fact, turned out to be their strong suit. Who would have known? They questioned everything and always kept an open mind. They took their time and never rushed into quick decisions, eventually finding their way forward once they both agreed on the next step. These practices turned out to be invaluable.

When Lambda Legal took the case, B and Kendall not only were blessed with incredible legal support, they also received some much-needed relief from the compounding legal costs as Lambda was taking the case pro bono. The women could now focus on chipping away at the legal expenses accrued from previous years without incurring additional costs. From that moment on, they both slept much better.

Over the following months, Jon Davidson and his colleagues at Lambda prepared the written opening and reply briefs for the appellate court. After the briefing was finished, Jon prepared oral arguments against BHCC to be delivered to the three appellate judges of the Fourth District Court of Appeal in San Diego. Since B and Kendall had lost the summary judgment that dismissed their case, the burden was on them to show why that court had erred in reaching the decision it had reached. Five months later, they found themselves sitting in the gallery watching Jon work his magic in front of the three appellate judges. Hearing someone of his caliber speaking on their behalf was an honor. When Jon spoke their names in that hallowed setting, it was difficult for B and Kendall to comprehend that he was referring to them. But he was. And he meant business.

In BHCC's rebuttal, they objected and said the couple's evidence was irrelevant or inadmissible. It was frustrating to watch John Shiner, the lead attorney for Morrison & Foerster, repeat during an oral argument that much of B and Kendall's evidence was just "nits in the wind." He clearly wanted to communicate that their evidence was about as impactful as tiny pests.

The judges vigorously disagreed. One of the judges commented: "Mr. Shiner, the statement in Mr. Jeffers's affidavit was from the general manager, not just any member. He was a person of authority for the club. I would not call that 'nits in the wind,' especially in light of the fact that you haven't provided an affidavit to dispute it."

While it felt good to hear the judge refute Mr. Shiner's argument, it also demonstrated that the club had not developed any more of a defense for their actions.

On March 8, 2004, the court concluded that:

> *Koebke and French presented sufficient evidence to raise a triable issue of material fact on their claim that Bernardo Heights Country Club applied its membership bylaws in a discriminatory manner by granting unmarried heterosexual couples family membership privileges while denying those same privileges to them,*

and, therefore, reverse the judgment entered in favor of BHCC as to this claim.

On the other hand, the court also concluded that:

> *BHCC's policies, as written, do not discriminate on the basis of gender or sexual orientation, only marital status. The Court concludes, applying the principles of the California Supreme Court's in Harris v. Capital Growth Investors XIV (12991) 52 Cal.3d 1142 (Harris), the Unruh Act does not preclude a country club from limiting membership benefits based upon marital status. We, the Court, therefore, uphold the lower court's summary adjudication of those claims and that portion of the judgment entered in BHCC's favor.*

It was a split decision! The appellate court had reversed the summary judgment. B and Kendall won the right to return to the lower court and move forward with their case to prove BHCC discriminated against them by treating them differently than some other single members at the club. So they could go to trial on those grounds.

However, this was not the reason they started the case. Their primary goal had been to be able to play golf together, without a guest fee, because they were family. But at least they would get their day in court to prove the club had discriminated against them.

Over time, B and Kendall felt more and more optimistic about a positive outcome. In addition, the onslaught of positive media attention following the reversal of their case surprised and encouraged them. After the article in *Golf for Women* and the couple's victory at the appellate court, the Golf Channel reached out to them with a request to do a story about their case. They agreed, and the network came to their home with a crew of five men, who spent a full weekend filming the story. Suddenly, media attention was overwhelming and heartening. *The Wall Street Journal* and *USA Today* featured their story, which was also covered by the *Los Angeles Times*, *The San Diego Union-Tribune*, and several other newspapers from across the state. TV stations up the coast of California also provided positive coverage of their case.

HBO came next, filming at B and Kendall's house and on location around San Diego for almost a week with correspondent Armen Keteyian. The resulting episode of *Real Sports with Bryant Gumbel* was the highlight.

All this attention caught the women totally by surprise. They were stunned to have so much positive coverage. After so many frustrating years of legal dead ends, they were buoyed by the support.

On an amusing side note, B and Kendall had agreed to go water skiing with a friend on San Diego Bay and wanted to cancel their plans due to HBO filming that week. The producer said, "No way! You girls go and ski and we'll rent a boat for the crew and follow you around the bay." So HBO rented a boat for their crew of five guys from New York, who chased the couple and their friend around the bay. At one point in the day, the bay got really rough. The group from New York, not being boat people, almost lost a crew member with his camera. Despite that, they seemed to enjoy themselves and laughed their heads off. Everyone made B and Kendall feel comfortable and at ease. The couple was being seen, treated, and presented as what they were—a family.

Of all the media, it was Logan Jenkins, a local columnist for *The San Diego Union-Tribune*, who really grasped what was at stake and said it best. In 2003, Logan wrote: "What a pathetic rub of the green it would be if the greatest contribution of Bernardo Heights to the game of golf is as a footnote in the history of gay rights." But that was still nothing more than a fantasy.

PERSONAL SPACE

COLLEGE AND CAREER—B

My parents had made it very clear, very early, that if I wanted to go to college, I would have to find a way to pay for it myself. In order to minimize expenses, I attended junior college for two years. I played on the tennis team and in my second year my doubles partner and I won our division at the Doubles Championship at the Junior College National Tennis Championship. With this accomplishment, I was granted a half tennis, half academic scholarship for the last two years of my college education. My spending money came from teaching tennis privately on weekends and after school. My parents were very practical. For example, on my twenty-first birthday they contributed two new front tires for my AMC Gremlin—a car I had paid for with money from babysitting and working in retail during my summers and breaks.

I lived with my parents and paid for graduate school by working for the college as an administrative assistant to the undergraduates. Every penny I ever received I worked for. I did it on my own. I will always be proud of that! My first job out of college was working at a resort as their director of activities. I then sold print advertising, then radio, and then I received two job offers from TV stations in San Diego to sell airtime. I chose CBS because I respected their news, prime time, and more mature audience. My salary was 100 percent commission. I stayed with CBS for thirty-six years until I retired. It was a great, stressful, and exciting career.

I earned a good living and at twenty-eight, put a deposit down on a small home in San Diego. Four years later, I joined Bernardo Heights Country Club. Four years later, I met Kendall.

CHAPTER ELEVEN

Request to Be Heard

2004

With the appellate court decision behind them, Kendall and B were dealing with a mixed bag of emotions. They were delighted that the club wasn't totally off the hook, but their primary goal of golfing at the club together as members still seemed to be dead in the water.

Lambda was clear that their role in the case was completed and they would be transferring the case back over to Lionel Price to litigate the discrimination case in the trial court. The appellate court reversal of the lower court's summary judgment essentially meant that the case was being sent back to the trial court on the merits of the discrimination claim. Lionel was the trial lawyer, Lambda handled the appellate part of the case, and Lionel would now be handling the case again.

Just after the appellate court's decision, Kendall and B went on a ski trip to Deer Valley with friends from Atlanta. It was a nice distraction from the angst they felt when they golfed, where the question always remained: Do they play at the club or play somewhere else less hostile and uncomfortable?

A few days into their ski trip, the women were on the chairlift heading in to meet their friends for lunch when Kendall's cell phone rang. They were both surprised to see Jon's name flash across the phone screen. Curious as to why he was calling, Kendall answered the phone while on the lift. Jon, with a cheery voice, asked if they had a minute—he wanted to run an idea by them. This man had earned far more than a minute. They carefully skied off the lift, Kendall's phone glued to her ear, as they looked for a good spot where they could put Jon on speaker so they both could hear his idea.

Jon shared that he had struggled with the decision made by the appellate court to uphold the summary judgment regarding BHCC's policy that discriminated on the basis of marital status. He went on to explain that, based on his research, there were conflicting decisions from various California appellate districts relative to cases affecting single people. He explained that not every case before the California Supreme Court has a clear ruling one way or another, so the court occasionally agrees to hear what is called a "request to be heard" case.

Jon went on to say it was a bit of a long shot, as the California Supreme Court decides to hear less than 10 percent of the cases submitted to it, but if B and Kendall were interested, it was worth a try. Jon reassured them that Lambda would again cover all legal expenses and that their work involved in filing a request to be heard would come at no cost to the couple. B and Kendall were truly elated that there was still a shot—albeit a long shot—at accomplishing the primary goal of the lawsuit: to not be discriminated against based on their family status. They wanted to play golf together as family members.

Over lunch, B and Kendall updated their friends about the exciting new development. They felt truly fortunate to be recipients of the dedication and genius of Jon Davidson. Over a couple glasses of wine, they talked with their friends about how crazy it was that what had appeared to be such a simple and straightforward case had now gone through four years of litigation. It had moved from a request to a complaint to a summary judgment in the lower court, then on to the Fourth Circuit Court of Appeal for a split decision that directed them back to the lower court, and now to the possibility of going before the California Supreme Court.

Just as the women had experienced in all other aspects of their lawsuit, there was a long period of silence as Jon worked on his request to be heard by the California Supreme Court. That was followed by another long period of silence, once their case was submitted, while they waited to hear whether or not the court would hear their case. The request to be heard would put the trial court discrimination case on hold. B and Kendall felt like they were sitting on a plane on the tarmac waiting to take off with an unknown departure time—indefinite waiting with no clue as to when the wait would end.

Because the women were busy with their careers, families, and day-to-day lives, the lawsuit seemed to fade away and life seemed somewhat normal again for several months while they awaited the next chapter in this complicated and lengthy battle.

When they received a call from Jon, it was out of the blue. He was ecstatic to share the great news—the California Supreme Court had agreed to hear their case! In California there was conflicting case law, so the court would hear B. Birgit Koebke and Kendall E. French vs. Bernardo Heights Country Club with the hope that their case would bring clarity for future cases that were similar. B and Kendall were beyond thrilled. They couldn't believe their good fortune—and they knew it wouldn't have happened without Jon.

For the couple, the gift of having Jon as their attorney was not only his phenomenal reputation, it was his ability to champion a case—and to build support around that case. Jon also had incredible knowledge and experience in this field, having coauthored the then-recently adopted California Domestic Partnership Law. As Jon prepared his brief for submission, he also worked hard to gather backing for their case through amicus briefs, also known as "friend of the court" briefs, which are legal documents filed in appellate court cases by non-litigants with a strong interest in the subject matter. The briefs advise the court of relevant additional information or arguments that the court might wish to consider.

When Jon finally filed the official brief to the California Supreme Court on B and Kendall's behalf, he had garnered support via amicus briefs from numerous organizations. The first amicus brief was filed by Bill Lockyer, then-attorney general for the state of California. It was followed by several others, including ACLU Foundation; ACLU of Northern California, ACLU of Southern California; ACLU of San Diego and Imperial Counties; Lesbian and Gay

Rights Foundation; the Anti-Defamation League; Equality California; Tom Homann LGBT Law Association; Women's Sports Foundation; California Women's Law Center; and National Center for Lesbian Rights.

Like much of the positive media attention the couple had experienced, it was vindicating for Kendall and B to have so many organizations supporting their case and believing in them to help right the wrongs they were fighting. It was also interesting to note the sheer lack of support BHCC received on what was, in the California Supreme Court's view, an inconclusive topic for which it hoped this case would provide clarity. No amicus briefs were filed to support BHCC's position. When Jon sent the couple a copy of the first amicus brief from Bill Lockyer, they were overwhelmed just reading his opening argument:

> *Treating registered domestic partners differently from married couples in the provision of any accommodation, advantage, facility, privilege, or service by a business establishment, without a legitimate business reason for such differentiation, is a violation of the Unruh Civil Rights Act.*

While Jon and the other organizations were preparing their briefs for B and Kendall, they were able, once again, to get back to life as usual. They were in the capable hands of Jon, who needed very little from them as this portion of the case was based on argument of the existing case law.

PERSONAL SPACE

SKIING

From Kendall: Not long after we had our first dinner date, B called to let me know she was going skiing and was thinking about inviting me but first wanted to confirm I was at least an intermediate skier. She wasn't interested in skiing with a beginner. I learned to ski at twelve and was a pretty good skier as a teen, but I gave it up when I started college. So when B asked what type of skier I was, I said, "I'm okay, but it's been a long time." Once, I had gone with a mutual friend, so B called our friend and she assured B that I was a good skier. So we drove the six hours to Mammoth and the moment of truth came: Can Kendall ski? I popped my skis on, hopped on the lift, and effortlessly skied off the chair with a quick shush of my skis. B had trouble keeping up with me on the slopes that day! To her credit, she was quick with a humble pie apology. All these years later, skiing at Mammoth is our favorite winter activity.

From B: Kendall is very good; I just try to keep up without falling. So Kendall has an app on her phone that's just for skiers. Once when we were relaxing after a day of skiing, I noticed on Kendall's phone app that she had posted a speed of 54 mph that day—while skiing! I wasn't happy and pleaded with her to slow down. Kendall agreed, albeit reluctantly, and I was relieved. After all, she needs to stay healthy so that we can keep skiing together as we age!

CHAPTER TWELVE

San Francisco

2005

The day the couple had been waiting for had finally come. Not just another day in another court—B and Kendall's day in the California Supreme Court. It was May 2005. Kendall and B packed their bags to fly to San Francisco to witness Jon Davidson argue B. Birgit Koebke and Kendall E. French vs. Bernardo Heights Country Club before the California Supreme Court—clearly a once-in-a-lifetime event. Kendall's mom, Truth, went along to savor the historic moment and offer moral support. They all were excited, of course, but wary at the same time. Truth offered much-needed motherly guidance, as she always did, and continued to be the voice of reason.

The women opted to stay in a small hotel; it felt warmer and more serene than a big-box hotel. They were heading into uncharted territory and wanted a cozy place that felt comforting. B, Kendall, and Truth were very close. Truth was their number one cheerleader and supporter. They loved having her by their side. No matter how old a child gets, there is nothing more empowering and comforting than a loving parent.

To make sure he was completely prepared for this unparalleled moment before the California Supreme Court, Jon Davidson had conducted his moot court in Los Angeles the week before. A moot court is a practice session for oral argument, where legal colleagues act as justices of the court and pepper the attorney with tough questions about their case and the applicable laws. Jon had arrived in San Francisco the day before the hearing to finish his last-minute prep work. B and Kendall knew they were in great hands.

After the trial court dismissed the case in 2002, Lambda Legal took over the case in both the California appellate court and the California Supreme Court. B and Kendall were entirely free of responsibility for all legal fees from that point on. What a relief!

The next morning, Truth, Kendall, and B were too nervous to eat breakfast, so they had coffee and then headed to the Earl Warren Building. The usual chatter among them had ceased as they were caught up in their own thoughts. What would it be like to sit in the state's highest court and hear the arguments from both sides? They knew the case would likely end here, but the question was *how*.

As the women approached the courthouse, they were mesmerized by the sheer size of the historic building, gleaming with pristine white stucco and church-like windows. The interior housed rich leather chairs and beautiful dark wood paneling. It was a place where one could easily feel underdressed or intimidated—but the three women were confidently clothed in their best business attire.

When B and Kendall's case was called up, they both felt anxious, not really knowing what to expect. Jon Davidson argued their case as the women sat motionless. Like a good tennis match, the arguments went back and forth. After half an hour, there was still no indication as to which way the decision would go. It felt endless. The couple was emotionally exhausted just watching.

The arguments concluded, and that night Kendall, B, and Truth felt they needed to celebrate this historic day with an evening out in the city. They dined at their favorite restaurant, Zuni Café, and savored their famous roasted chicken with bread salad. Win or lose, they toasted each other with a champagne cocktail, Truth's favorite—the perfect ending to a perfect day. With great optimism, they boarded the plane the next morning, still reveling in the experience.

For the next three months, time passed rapidly for Kendall. She started a new job with GlaxoSmithKline Pharmaceuticals as a sales professional and had spent most of the summer training in North Carolina. But for B, time dragged on while she waited for the ruling on the case. She flew to Austin for a speaking engagement for Lambda Legal. She hoped the long weekend in Texas without Kendall would make the time pass faster. At work, she kept herself as busy as possible, taking on new projects.

On August 1, 2005, the California Supreme Court issued a ruling in B and Kendall's case. Justice Carlos R. Moreno wrote the majority opinion for the court:

> *While creating a family-friendly environment may be a legitimate business interest, that policy is not served when a business discriminates against the domestic partner of one of its members. Rather, by so doing, the*

> *business violated the policy favoring domestic partnerships which, like the policy favoring marriage, seeks to promote families as well as reduce discrimination based on gender and sexual orientation.*

In the roughly three months between when their case was heard and when the decision came down, one of the seven justices had retired. Jon Davidson summarized it best:

> *The majority opinion was joined by five justices. One justice agreed in part with the decision and disagreed in part. The majority held that if a business in California denies registered domestic partners benefits it grants to married couples, the business has engaged in marital status discrimination, violating California's public accommodations nondiscrimination law (known as the Unruh Act). This was the first California Supreme Court opinion to decide that the Unruh Act prohibits marital status discrimination and to hold that businesses must treat registered domestic partners the same as they treat spouses. The California Supreme Court therefore reversed the judgment of the lower court ruling against B and Kendall and held that, going forward, the country club could not treat B and Kendall worse than married couple members. The majority further held that there was sufficient evidence that, even before the effective date of California's comprehensive registered domestic partnership law, the country club was enforcing its rules about who besides a member could use the club without paying fees and could use it more than a limited*

number of times each year in a discriminatory fashion, entitling B and Kendall with the right to prove that this occurred and to recover damages for that earlier conduct. The one justice who wrote separately (agreeing in part and disagreeing in part with the majority) agreed with the first part of the majority's conclusions but would have gone further in holding that the club was engaging in discrimination prior to that because B and Kendall were registered domestic partners under the earlier, less comprehensive domestic partnership law of California. They also would have allowed claims for sexual orientation discrimination to go forward, given the evidence that existed of anti-lesbian comments by club members.

Lambda Legal, under the brilliant guidance of Jon Davidson, scored a big victory on B and Kendall's behalf and on behalf of the tens of thousands of domestic partnerships in California. The ruling assured that domestic partners, regardless of gender or sexual orientation, had to be afforded *all* of the same considerations as a married couple.

Kendall and B were both at work when Jon Davidson called them with the incredible news. Finally, an enormous step forward! They were thrilled that the courts recognized that couples with a domestic partnership, like Kendall and B, now had to be treated the same as married couples by all businesses in California. They rushed home and opened a bottle of champagne to celebrate. After all these years, all the turmoil, the lost friends, the alienation, the heartache, and the financial loss, they finally had something to show for it.

Since the California Supreme Court ruling was based on the Domestic Partnership Act, which became effective January 2005, the couple was entitled to receive just seven months of legal expense reimbursement from BHCC, which covered the period from January to August 2005. Although they were thrilled to have such an important victory, and Lambda Legal had made the impact they were seeking, the ruling did little to help B and Kendall recoup the legal costs and monthly club dues and fees they had incurred over the previous four years.

In August of 2005, Logan Jenkins with *The San Diego Union-Tribune* wrote:

> *The Supreme Court took note and cut off the legal branch from which Bernardo Heights was hanging. Unless the club defies the court, which appears unlikely, Koebke and French should be free to tee whenever they feel like it. No more galling greens fees for French. In a pathetic rub of the green, Bernardo Heights has made civil rights history. Even if the course is bulldozed tomorrow and houses are built on its fairways, the club will end as a legal footnote. Now, I'm not advocating a gay pride tournament with rainbow-colored golf carts, but if it wants to end the costly bleeding, Bernardo Heights should graciously welcome Koebke and French as a family in good standing, and settle the original lawsuit without further acrimony.*

On September 12, 2005, just five weeks after the California Supreme Court decision came down, the couple received new BHCC ID cards—one for B and one for Kendall. They went to the club the same weekend to play a quiet round of golf—no guest registration, no additional fees, no welcome banner. The members continued to ignore them and went out of their way to avoid them entirely.

The staff at the club, however, welcomed them warmly, from the pro shop to the restaurant. It was terrific. They had known most of the staff for over ten years and their support was nothing short of heartwarming. They felt they had really accomplished something significant and hoped that, after a little time, the members might come around as well. That hope faded quickly as they realized how deep the hostility had become. Years ago, the members had ruined any sense of community and camaraderie that would normally come with joining a country club. At this point, the women really didn't care anymore.

Playing eighteen holes of golf under a family membership made B and Kendall feel vindicated and free. Life felt lighter than it had for a very long time. B shot an 81 and Kendall had six pars, which made for a magnificent day. They went inside, sat at the bar, and each had a martini followed by the best burger in town.

The following week, HBO *Real Sports* filmed a follow-up segment after the California Supreme Court ruling, joining B and Kendall on their vacation in New England. Armen Keteyian wanted to discuss what the ruling meant to them and to the tens of thousands of other Californians who were positively impacted.

Walking on the beach a few weeks later, B and Kendall noticed strangers waving, smiling, and giving them thumbs-up. They found out that the segment on HBO had been repeated that morning and people recognized them. What a nice contrast to the treatment they had received from the BHCC members! Public support was a lovely gesture, much needed after this long battle. They were starting to feel whole again.

It was a great time—but B and Kendall knew they had one more big fight ahead of them.

CHAPTER THIRTEEN

Another Setback

2006

In August 2006, a year after the California Supreme Court ruling, B and Kendall traveled to Chicago to participate in the Gay Games golf event. While there, they reached out to Mary Fechtig, a lawyer, dear friend, and terrific golfer who had played competitively for Indiana University. They shared their concerns that the club was not initiating any settlement discussions regarding the discrimination case that was now remanded back to the trial court on the merits following the favorable California Supreme Court ruling. Now that the appellate process had been resolved in their favor, Lambda Legal was no longer representing them and they were back in the hands of their original trial lawyer, Lionel Price.

Based on their supreme court victory, Mary was concerned that the couple had not yet entered into any meaningful settlement negotiations. She wanted to look into their case further and help them out if possible, but first she needed to check with her DC law firm, Zuckerman Spaeder, to see if they would permit her to work with the couple pro bono. She insisted they should not have to pay any more money in fees, because she felt they had already done their part. They were grateful to have someone they trusted offer real insight into where their case was headed. Mary followed up with the good news that she obtained approval from her law firm to work toward a settlement on their case pro bono. Hallelujah! They welcomed that development.

In previous years when B and Kendall were represented only by Lionel, they had participated in a settlement conference with the BHCC's legal team. During that meeting, the BHCC team walked out, leaving B, Kendall, and Lionel dumbfounded. After seeing Lambda Legal in action and talking with Mary, the women knew they had now benefited from the very best in lawyering. Jon Davidson had always been fully prepared and professional. Mary agreed to help them manage the settlement and to prepare for trial, if necessary. However, she was not licensed to practice law in the state of California, so she could support them only in an advisory capacity—she could not formally represent them. Therefore, B and Kendall decided to continue with Lionel as their attorney of record and Mary as an adviser.

Mary flew to San Diego where she, B, and Kendall had a conference with Lionel at his office. B and Kendall were firm with him that Mary's participation was essential. In Mary, they had someone they could trust to help them figure out the settlement value of the case versus the additional cost and risk of trial. They had been living with this lawsuit for almost seven years—far too long. They hoped that Mary's expertise in settling cases for insurance companies would help them negotiate a settlement.

Kendall and B were concerned that Lionel might be resistant to the added support Mary would provide. But he seemed appreciative and welcoming of the additional resources and help Mary could bring to the case. He delivered some preliminary information Mary needed to start preparing for a potential settlement conference.

It was once again the time of year for B's company, CBS 8, to take clients on the annual incentive trip. That year's thank-you to clients was going to be a trip to a truly thrilling destination—Russia. The clients would be accompanied by executives and two salespeople. B had worked hard all year to earn a spot. She and Kendall were thrilled that B's sales efforts qualified her to join the trip. They had now been on five other incentive trips with CBS 8 as a couple and knew the trips were always exciting and a lot of fun. And both had always wanted to travel to Russia.

Unfortunately, the timing was bad. The club proposed a date for the settlement conference that fell right in the middle of their trip. They debated back and forth whether to stay or go. Mary reassured them that they should go, and that she would attend the settlement conference to back up Lionel. After much deliberation and many reservations, B and Kendall decided to go on the trip. They knew it would be an experience they could not duplicate on their own. During B's thirty-six years with CBS 8, she had attended twenty-five of these incredible adventures. They were a credit to her excellent job performance and afforded her and Kendall a special perk of amazing experiences together. They cherished these trips, always felt welcome and accepted, and developed deep relationships with B's clients and coworkers—many who still remain dear friends.

The Russia trip was spectacular. On their final night in Saint Petersburg, the group was treated to dinner at Yusupov Palace, where Rasputin was assassinated. Later, the Bolshoi Ballet performed a private recital in the castle's stunning theater, and guests were treated to a piano recital by a child prodigy on the level of a young Lang Lang. The finale was a private fireworks display in front of the palace, over the Moika River. B and Kendall still reflect on this magical night all these years later. And to think they almost didn't go.

When the couple landed at LAX, they raced through the airport to charge their cell phones so they could speak to Mary about the settlement conference. As soon as she picked up, they were snapped back to reality. They could tell from Mary's first words that it did not go well: "Thank God you're back."

Mary relayed that the morning of the meeting with the club, Lionel had called her at the last minute, saying he had a filing due and she would have to handle the settlement conference on her own. Mary had no choice but to face BHCC, their attorneys, and their insurance company alone.

What Mary took away from the settlement meeting was that B and Kendall were in trouble. She realized why BHCC was in no hurry to settle—B and Kendall lacked specific compelling evidence. Mary saw their case as paper thin and believed they had only about a 50 percent chance of winning at trial. An actual settlement was not likely—one doesn't win a settlement; they are voluntary. The stronger the case is for one side, the more likely it is the other side will want to settle and pay money to avoid the risks of trial.

While B and Kendall appreciated and respected Mary's candor, this new revelation hit them like a punch in the gut. Mary had been insistent that the California Supreme Court was extremely specific in its ruling and in sending the discrimination portion of the case back to the trial court for a determination on the merits. Yes, it held that discrimination against domestic partners by a private country club was illegal in California, and now the trial court had to hold a full trial to determine if such discrimination occurred. B and Kendall had to present their case to a judge or jury proving that they were, in fact, treated differently than others.

The supreme court provided the roadmap needed to win the discrimination portion of the case, which, if the couple could prove discrimination, would likely lead to a monetary settlement. B and Kendall needed that settlement to recoup the money they had already spent—not just the legal fees for the last five years, but also the ongoing BHCC membership dues of over $750 that they had to keep paying each month so that B would continue to have standing in the lawsuit. The ball was now in their court to prove that BHCC had one set of rules for them and another set of rules for other members. The evidence they had gathered over the years—the guest books, fake sons and wives, and Court Bolton's statement about how other unmarried couples were treated—wasn't enough. They were stunned. No wonder BHCC was not interested in settling this case. They still insisted they hadn't done anything discriminatory.

B and Kendall were back at square one. Little did they know that what felt like a huge setback was actually a blessing in disguise.

After they had had a good night's sleep and were feeling better, the couple sat over coffee and discussed their situation.

Kendall was very concerned they would lose at trial. She knew it would be beyond devastating for B after all the friendships and money she had lost, and all the heartache. Kendall could picture the club taking a victory lap, the board members pounding their chests: "See, we didn't do anything wrong—the laws changed."

Kendall told B she had a bad feeling and did not agree that they should press forward with a trial. She didn't care if they settled for a hundred dollars. If they lost, B would never be the same—and there was no money worth that. If B insisted on going to trial, Kendall was out. She couldn't be part of it. If the trial went the way she suspected it would, she couldn't forgive herself for participating in something that hurt her partner. B was so passionate about the case that she didn't appear to be objective and didn't see the warning signs in front of them—but Kendall did.

The next day, the couple had another conversation with Mary. They agreed that they could see the importance of building a stronger case. They were obsessed with locating more compelling evidence for the trial. The stronger their case looked heading to trial, the more likely it was that BHCC would be willing to settle out of court to avoid an adverse verdict.

One Saturday morning, B and Kendall met with Lionel at his office. They asked what his strategy would be to obtain the additional evidence needed to settle the case. He insisted that wasn't necessary, saying a jury would like the women, trust them, see their side, and would be able to connect the dots with the evidence they did have. At one point he became agitated, pounding his fist on the conference table and saying, "We have what we have" and "There is no smoking gun."

It seemed to us Lionel clearly wanted to go to trial no matter what. But given the events over the past couple of weeks, Kendall did not want to go to trial under any circumstances. Over all the years of litigation, there was still no incriminating evidence. BHCC hadn't been convinced to settle. B and Kendall would now be relying on Lionel's strategy that depended on the jury liking and being sympathetic toward them to win this case.

As is her nature, B wanted to keep fighting. For the first time in their lawsuit, the two women differed on strategy. During all these years, as a couple and as a team, they had held together strongly. This time, however, Kendall was insistent with B, saying: "If by chance we lose in court, you will never be the same. And if we lose, this part is what people will remember."

B knew Kendall was right on both counts. If they lost in court, people would only remember that BHCC had done nothing wrong—and strengthening the Domestic Partnership Act would be a forgotten footnote. To her credit, B set aside her instincts to keep fighting and agreed that going to trial was not an option.

As in a lot of relationships, there is often a good cop and a bad cop. B, with her straightforward style, sometimes appearing aggressive or abrasive, was usually the bad cop. Growing up as a bit of a beach girl, Kendall was typically diplomatic and easygoing whenever there was tension. Usually, she was the first to jump in and smooth things over—but this time was different. She raised her voice to Lionel for the very first time.

"Lionel, we're going to dot every I, cross every T, and pursue every avenue we can find to strengthen our case in an attempt to get a reasonable settlement," Kendall said. "Win or lose, we have to know that we exhausted every possible avenue to get the best outcome while avoiding trial." The meeting adjourned quickly after that. B and Kendall drove back to their house in silence.

When they got home, they called Mary. The three agreed again that they didn't yet have strong enough evidence to feel confident in mitigating the risk of an unfavorable outcome at the trial court. They were very nervous about going to trial and taking a chance that they could lose. Not at this point. They had come too far. The supreme court's ruling provided B and Kendall with the ability to play golf together under a family membership, winning the most significant aspect of their lawsuit. Fighting BHCC now for the discrimination they endured at the club didn't seem to be such a high bar to reach. Jon Davidson also felt a settlement should not be difficult to reach after their victory. That's why the couple felt it was appropriate to pursue the discrimination case, going back to the lower court.

Our sense was that the Bernardo Heights Country Club Board was still insisting they had not been discriminatory in any way. And it appeared they were trying to convince the BHCC members that B and Kendall got lucky with the California Supreme Court ruling and had won only because the law had changed. They still maintained that they had done nothing wrong and were simply following their bylaws. B and Kendall had to find incriminating evidence—the smoking gun. That was the only way to settle this case and move on with their lives.

PERSONAL SPACE

DOGS

On a special vacation in Salzburg, Austria, we started noticing people inside and outside of restaurants, having dinner or cake and coffee, with their small dogs sitting under the table. These charming scenes really warmed our hearts.

Soon after we returned home, we went on the hunt for a small dog of our own. We decided on a dachshund to remind us of our wonderful time in Salzburg. We named the dog Mozart—go figure. Sadly, we lost Mozart after twelve years. We now have Patron and Mavrik, the sweetest little Chihuahuas in the world. The pups are "brothers from another mother" and add lots of joy and laughter to our home.

CHAPTER FOURTEEN

Epiphany

2006

The months following the decision by the California Supreme Court were a time of intense mixed feelings. The court had ruled that the BHCC had discriminated against B and Kendall as registered domestic partners. However, it did not decide whether the couple had been discriminated against prior to 1999, the year that domestic partnership was established under state law.

Lambda Legal had donated their legal expertise and advanced all costs for the Fourth District Court of Appeal and California Supreme Court. However, B and Kendall had paid tens of thousands of dollars of legal fees and costs prior to Lambda's involvement.

Lionel Price felt there was "no smoking gun" in the evidence prior to 2001 or during the numerous years of litigation with the club that would push BHCC to a favorable settlement. However, Kendall rightfully insisted that a trial was too risky. She and B, having lived through those years of discrimination, felt that evidence must exist and they could find it if they turned over every rock.

At BHCC, Kendall could now play golf as much as she wanted under the couple's family membership, but at this time she was focusing on training for her new job. B would have been happy to just leave BHCC as all the members—even her former Cronies—had shunned her anyway, but she had to stay, even play alone, in order to maintain a legal standing until a settlement was reached on the discrimination portion.

Because the laws had changed and strengthened their domestic partnership, the women could now join any club they wished. Their domestic partnership was equal to a marriage license, according to the California Supreme Court ruling. But all the years of hurt, disappointment, and frustration—not to mention all the acrimony and expense—could have been avoided if BHCC had granted their simple request to provide Kendall with guest passes. No legal fees would have been incurred by either party. No trials. No landmark rulings. B and Kendall had to keep reminding themselves that this situation wasn't just about a game of golf anymore.

Despite their mixed emotions, the couple was grateful for the support they had received from Lambda Legal and for their ability to return to a sense of normalcy in their daily lives. Both before and after their appeals, B and Kendall made many public appearances on behalf of Lambda Legal. It was gratifying for them to assist Lambda by speaking about their case at fundraising events. B and Kendall were often the featured speakers. Jon Davidson would tee up their talk. Then they would share how the case had impacted their lives—the sadness of losing friends for simply speaking up against a double standard, and the powerlessness they had felt before Lambda Legal's involvement, when they had been completely outlawyered against a full team of BHCC lawyers.

These appearances were truly win-win-win events: B and Kendall really enjoyed meeting the people, who were always welcoming, smart, kind, and caring. Lambda Legal benefited from the donors who wanted to get behind a case like theirs to fight discrimination. And the donors were able to see first-hand how their contributions to Lambda Legal were making a difference in the lives of ordinary people.

On this day, as B and Kendall were driving to Los Angeles for another Lambda Legal speaking engagement, they were quiet with their own thoughts. About an hour into the drive, they started discussing the case and the importance of finding truly compelling evidence. They started focusing on the BHCC members who had a phony son or a wink-and-nod wife, trying to figure out where and how they could find additional evidence of discrimination.

Suddenly, Kendall blurted out, "Hey, what was it your friend Megan said about the folks at BHCC 'rushing to the altar' after our supreme court ruling?"

Megan was a member of another private country club in the area. She and B had been friends since their twenties. They were both tennis instructors in Rancho Bernardo and gave private lessons. Rancho Bernardo is a bedroom community with many 55+ neighborhoods, and people talk.

"Oh, yeah," said B. "Megan called me and said, 'I keep hearing rumors that members from Bernardo Heights are rushing to the altar. What's up with that?' I didn't give it much thought; I just thought it was kind of funny at the time."

The two looked at each other, suddenly energized. Could they be on to something?

"Let's figure out exactly what she meant!" said Kendall decisively.

B and Kendall knew it was critical to follow up on this revelation immediately but weren't sure how to proceed. Though there was a difference of opinion if we would prevail in a trial. This was the difference between the women and Lionel Price: regardless of what happened at trial, Lionel would collect his fees and move on to his next case. But B and Kendall would have to live the rest of their lives with the outcome. B and Kendall felt strongly they needed to take control of this aspect of their case. If they could find compelling evidence that would lead to a settlement in their favor, at the end of the day the victory would be theirs and Lambda Legal's legacy would endure.

On the drive home that night from Los Angeles, the couple formulated a plan to follow up on their new opportunity. They had found a potential lifeline and their combined newfound energy was revitalizing.

CHAPTER FIFTEEN

Smoking Gun

2006

Just a few miles from her office, B entered the clubhouse during her lunch break the following day. She started looking around the ladies' locker room for the most recently updated membership roster. Passing her own locker, she suddenly felt nostalgic about how cool she once thought it was. Sure, she had had a locker in school with a metal door and a number on it. But this locker was dark wood and had a gold nameplate at the top inscribed with her full name. Viewing this now only brought back the pain and disappointment the club had needlessly put her through.

After much hunting, B found the current year's roster near the spot where members posted their daily score. It contained the full names and addresses of all the members of the club. No one was in the locker room, so B quickly put it in her pocket and walked out to her car—excited and sad at the same time. She felt much like Inspector Clouseau, having found the first clue that might solve her and Kendall's mystery.

That night, Kendall and B discussed their strategy. How could they determine if everyone on the roster with a family membership was actually married at the time of their BHCC membership application? After much brainstorming, they realized they could research marriage licenses at the county clerk's office to determine the actual date of the marriages.

For the next week, during their lunchtime, the women met at the county clerk's office in downtown San Diego. They were on a great hunt for marriage license records of members with a family membership who claimed they were married when, in fact, they were not. Because of the rumor that several couples had "rushed to the altar" after the California Supreme Court victory in 2005, they needed to find at least one couple who had knowingly been permitted by the club to falsely pose as married both before and after their initial lawsuit.

The club roster was alphabetized, so B and Kendall sat at the county computers and started with the As, checking to see which couples were unmarried during the years of their lawsuit—from 2001 through 2005. The process was tedious and tiresome. After the first five days working through their lunchtime, they decided to speed things up by taking a few vacation days from work so they could spend entire days on research. Now, they were the first to arrive each morning when the clerk's office opened. They would pack their lunch and a few snacks and go through county marriage records every day for the next several days. Working very patiently and methodically, they developed a streamlined system that included double-checking every name to make sure nothing fell through the cracks.

Each day, Kendall and B would take an hour break and walk to the scenic San Diego harbor to recharge. With the wake from small boats gently crashing against the rocks, they would share smiles and waves with passengers sailing by. Cruise ships and aircraft carriers lined the ports on either side of the bay, with the picturesque Coronado Bridge and downtown skyline as a perfect backdrop. As they were strolling along the harbor's edge to the Star of India and passing all the docked boats bobbing in the water, they felt so fortunate to live in this beautiful city. San Diego weather is among the best in the country and truly suits the couple's outdoor lifestyle.

Back at the clerk's office, the women would sometimes make a game of the monotonous process to help the time pass. They both believed this was their last chance to vindicate themselves and prove that the club had turned a blind eye to straight couples pretending to be married while at the same time subjecting B and Kendall to extreme scrutiny. Although they laughed a lot during this project, they took it very seriously.

Legal claims of discrimination don't require proof of a pattern of discrimination: just *one incident* would be sufficient if it demonstrated that the club treated B and Kendall differently from other couples in similar circumstances. That meant they only needed to find one couple who played golf as family members but were not actually married at the time. And the evidence of discrimination that would pack the most power would be if that one couple was in a sham marriage during their years of litigation.

Logic would suggest that it would be prudent for a club being sued for discrimination against an unmarried gay couple to ensure that all prospective members applying for family memberships were, in fact, married—especially during the time of the discrimination lawsuit. Common sense, right? A simple request to see prospective members' marriage licenses would be the most logical step for the club to take during the period of the litigation, since it was the one document Kendall and B could not provide. But did they request that? No, they did not.

During their first full day of research, Kendall and B found the first potential marriage impostors who had been playing under a family membership as a married couple for several years but did not actually get married until 2004. The women exchanged high fives, hugged each other tight, and kept searching for more. The next day, they found four more marriage licenses for couples who were likely impostors because they had been playing as a family before the date of their marriages. The search was getting very exciting.

On the final day, the women found two more marriages within the 2001 to 2005 time frame. Although they were fairly certain these couples were not marriage impostors, to leave no rock unturned, they paid to have those marriage licenses copied too.

Kendall and B were beyond excited. They knew in their gut they were on to something big. Could they have finally found proof of what they had suspected all these years? For all the hours of billable hours, it looked like they were going to be the ones to find the necessary evidence that would lead to a satisfactory settlement of their case. The records of marriage licenses felt like a huge lifeline. They now had something tangible to work with. Each night they came home from their research exhausted, yet hopeful. Surely, all the lunch hours and vacation days they invested would pay off and identify at least one couple who had a family membership and was posing as married but was not.

Years earlier, as part of discovery, Lionel had requested the BHCC membership applications for all its members. The club always stonewalled him, arguing that the request was too broad. In all fairness, it *was* broad. After all, there were 320 membership files. And if BHCC had turned them over at the beginning of the lawsuit, Lionel, B, and Kendall would not have known what to look for. Nevertheless, the club always seemed to get away with stalling. But now that they had the marriage licenses of several couples they suspected had rushed to the altar, they knew exactly which membership files they needed to request.

Kendall and B presented the copies of the marriage licenses to Lionel. After reviewing this newly found evidence, Lionel sent a formal request to BHCC for twenty-four couples' membership files. Unlike before, this request for a reasonable number of membership files was not too broad. Not surprisingly, the club continued to stonewall and fight the discovery request. Only after the presiding judge ordered them to do so did the club finally release the files. Kendall and B were really only interested in ten files but had decided to ask for twenty-four so as not to tip their hand.

After receiving the files, they started reviewing the applications with a laser focus. They had to determine when the members joined the club as a stated married couple versus when they actually married. They learned BHCC had admitted several couples as members before they were married—and admitted these members without requesting any proof of their marriage certificate, even during the years of their lawsuit!

Kendall and B spread the BHCC membership files and the marriage license copies out over the conference room table, trying to keep both sets of files in order. The conference room was so quiet they could hear each other breathing. They then compared the marriage licenses to the members' original applications.

They found that during the years of their lawsuit, four of the nine couples they identified as suspicious had lied on their application for family membership and were not married as they had claimed. They only needed *one* instance for the purpose of their lawsuit but found *four*. They were elated by their discovery and could only imagine how many other marriage impostors they would find before 2001. But they kept their focus on 2001–2005, during the lawsuit. There it was—incriminating evidence of the club's discriminatory double standard—and Kendall and B had discovered it without the help of any lawyers. The club had asked for proof of marriage only from them because they knew it was impossible to provide. And the club either did not ask or looked the other way in these four instances with heterosexual couples. The club's decision to not require applicants to show proof of marriage had backfired.

Once again, this finding was a very clear signal that the club was not taking the lawsuit seriously and that it had a definite double standard. They were fine with admitting unmarried couples without bothering to ask for a copy of a marriage license—but for a gay couple, a marriage license was required. To us, they did not want to give family membership privileges to gay couples. It was as simple as that.

Busted! Smoking gun found!

This was truly the single most important lesson of the entire lawsuit: it was imperative that B and Kendall regain control of their destiny. Had they not been proactive in finding their own evidence, it's very unlikely they could have settled with BHCC when they lacked actual hard evidence. The judge or jury could have tossed their case at trial if they hadn't had strong proof of discrimination. But they knew they had found their much-needed evidence. Now the women were finally in a strong position to settle this case in their favor to avoid the uncertainty of a trial. Their strategy had worked. They could not have been more overjoyed.

It was time for a meaningful mediation session.

PERSONAL SPACE
FRIDAY DATE NIGHTS

On Fridays, our official date night, we always rush home from wherever we are and meet at our living room bar by 6:00 p.m. We sit and catch up, discussing our week over a cocktail and a light dinner. We have always done this and it is still the highlight of the week. Kendall, an aspiring mixologist, often has a new drink she wants to try, and B is always happy to be the guinea pig. We've kept this ritual for over thirty years. It is our time to reconnect. Our friends and family know that very few things in our lives can preempt our special Friday date night routine.

Originally, our bar was a typical tract home bar that would accommodate two people with a step-down for the server. When we remodeled, Kendall lobbied enthusiastically for a much bigger, more contemporary bar that could seat up to ten people. Our bar is now the focal point of the house and features a ridiculous selection of spirits. Kendall had even filmed a monthly cocktail-of-the-month episode at the bar for a lifestyle TV show called the *Daily Flash* when we're not traveling. And when we travel to a fun place and a cocktail inspires Kendall, we would film on location. In 2019, we filmed six episodes out of the country from Belfast to Punta Mita. The show airs on networks across the US and reaches about one million viewers.

The funny part about having a bar with a personal mixologist is that B only drinks one drink—cosmopolitans. Recently, she added mai tais to her list—but just to be clear, Kendall does make a perfect cosmo! She knows just what B likes and that she is a creature of habit. And here's a fun fact about B: She has driven the same car for over twenty years. After all, "It still runs great and looks great! Why mess with perfection?"

CHAPTER SIXTEEN

Mediation

2007

As the trial was approaching, the presiding judge pushed both sides for one last settlement conference. This time, the mediation would be held before a sitting judge. Kendall and B believed an actual judge would be more likely to assess the merits of the case at trial and push both sides to settle based on the likely outcome of a trial. In the past, mediators had not really done a deep dive into the merits or pushed hard to get the case settled.

What they also knew was that, for the first time, they were entering a mediation session prepared and armed with incriminating evidence. BHCC continued to hang on to their talking point: "We did nothing wrong; the law changed giving benefits to domestic partnerships." Thus, they claimed they did not owe the couple anything. The problem with that argument was that, before the law changed, the club did, in fact, discriminate against B and Kendall because they were gay. And now they had actual evidence to prove it.

This case was never about money. Kendall and B were patient and reasonable people. They had offered cost-free solutions to the club for many years. BHCC had done everything in their power to keep them out. Kendall and B had done everything to not let the club get away with treating them as undesirables and dismissing them, while making accommodations for other unmarried couples. They fought for seven years and held their heads high under the most extreme circumstances. It felt like every member at the club was against the couple for no valid reason other than the club's unwillingness to admit that they were wrong.

The settlement conference was set for Wednesday, January 3, 2007, in the San Diego County Courthouse. Kendall and B were relieved that Mary was flying in from Chicago to help with what they hoped would be the final mediation.

Through numerous conversations, it was clear that the four were in sync with all facets of the case and all felt confident that a positive outcome was imminent. They knew they had strong evidence going in. The facts and evidence put them in the driver's seat for the first time. They carried a bright red folder containing the marriage licenses, guarding them at this point as if they were made of gold. B held the folder so tight, the red ink printed on the front bled all over her sweating hands.

On the day of the mediation, Kendall and B arrived at 8:00 a.m. and sat in the judge's office adjoining his chambers for the entire day. Unfortunately, they were not allowed to be a part of the settlement negotiations in the judge's chambers, but Lionel and Mary were like tennis balls bouncing in and out to speak to the couple about potential settlements. They also went at least a half dozen times between the judge and the representatives for Bernardo Heights—each time, the club offered a different settlement figure.

Kendall and B's process was similar. To come up with a number that was worth the seven years of hell they had been put through, they did all the calculations. They factored in how much was owed to Lionel and a donation for Lambda, including all outstanding bills and all the monthly BHCC dues B had paid during the lawsuit years. Mary's presence gave Kendall and B an added layer of comfort and confidence about their not being able to sit in on the mediation.

Being armed with the evidence of the marriage licenses, it was only a matter of time before this case would finally settle without going to trial. Finally, at 8:00 p.m., a settlement was reached that was acceptable to everyone. Kendall and B's recent discovery of the marriage licenses had made it impossible for the judge to consider their mistreatment by the club as "nits in the wind" as BHCC's legal representative, John Shiner, had once stated. They all stayed late while the judge wrote up the agreement. Kendall and B felt that the judge had their best interests at heart, and that he supported settling the case, once and for all.

To say the couple was relieved to have this behind them is a huge understatement. B remembers sitting in the judge's chambers at the end of evening with Kendall by her side, almost numb, yet so overcome with relief that she could burst. Kendall's smile signaled that she felt the same. They both let out a huge sigh, tears in their eyes, as they were overcome with gratitude. The realization that their years-long ordeal was finally over, and they had attained their desired outcome, felt almost too good to be true. Mary was delighted with the results as well.

After B and Kendall signed the final paperwork, they decided to celebrate by going out to dinner and toasting this amazing day. Without the compelling evidence, the settlement might have been zero. Even with it, there was no guarantee a trial would have gone their way. B and Kendall considered it to be a perfect outcome: a big win and a happy ending to a seemingly unwinnable case.

CHAPTER SEVENTEEN

History Class

2020

Thirteen years later, B was spending the morning with her ninety-five-year-old father, as she usually did when she and Kendall (now her wife) weren't traveling. Now that the women were both retired, they had the luxury of time. After cake and coffee and visiting with her father, B left to spend the rest of the day with the three godchildren she and Kendall share. With no children of their own, having a close relationship with their godchildren was a lovely addition to their lives.

This particular Wednesday, their goddaughter Dillan, a sixteen-year-old high school junior, was excited to share a story from school. With excitement in her voice, Dillan said to B, "My government history teacher talked about you and Kendall in school today."

Okay Dillan, B thought, *you have my attention.* "What did he say?" B asked.

"We were studying supreme court cases that had an impact on society. My teacher talked about anti-slavery cases in the 1800s, then the Rosa Parks case in 1954, followed by McCulloch vs. Maryland, Madison vs. Madison, and many more. Then he discussed a case in California he felt significantly helped the fight for equal marriage rights—and it was *your* case, Koebke and French vs. Bernardo Heights! He said your case had a big impact on the forward movement of gay marriage rights in the United States."

It was clear this experience had caught Dillan totally off guard. B imagined Dillan, the daughter of two moms, sitting up a little taller in class. Her history class had now become real and personal to her. B was a little surprised as well, to be honest. Driving home that evening, she found herself sitting up a little taller in her car too.

After arriving home and sharing Dillan's announcement with Kendall, B became very curious about just how much impact they actually had made with their seven-year legal battle for equal rights at the Bernardo Heights Country Club. She and Kendall reaffirmed that the outcome had been worth the fight. They discovered their case had been cited in ninety-six appellate decisions, thirty-three law review articles, and at least 253 appellate or trial court briefs. Though their focus had been on simply wanting to play golf together and to be treated fairly by the club, they quickly learned this fight was about so much more than that.

The institution of marriage is often taken for granted. There are more than 1,100 statutory provisions that were not available to B and Kendall or any other same-sex couple who wanted the same benefits, rights, and privileges as heterosexual couples. These rights were a key factor in the debate over federal recognition of same-sex marriage. They include hospital visitation rights; inheritance of property; social security pensions; joint adoption; funeral and bereavement leave; joint filing of taxes; spousal privilege in court; survivor benefits; insurance licenses, coverages, and eligibility; property tax exemptions; supplemental security income; making spousal medical decisions; veterans disability; Medicaid; income tax deductions; disability payments for federal employees; and so many more.

B and Kendall had known the significance of what was being argued from the moment the California Supreme Court agreed to hear the case and from the moment Jon Davidson and Lambda began to discuss handling the initial appeal in the Fourth District Court of Appeal. They knew of its potential gravity, conceptually. They talked about it numerous times. But seeing its impact and hearing from people was surreal. For example, a short time after the California Supreme Court ruling, they were looking into refinancing their home, and the lender was talking about new legislation and a recent court case that significantly changed how the industry looks at domestic partners qualifying for loans. The lender had no idea he was talking to the couple whose names were on the case he was discussing! Lenders now take not just one but both borrowers' financial information into consideration if they have a domestic partnership agreement.

The couple received many letters of support and various golf invitations from around the country, which were touching gestures. The Nike Golf division sent a congratulatory golf package. People they had not heard from in years came out of the woodwork with praise and support.

B received a phone call from a long-lost friend from grade school, now director of human resources at a large firm in California. She wanted to tell B and Kendall what a huge difference they had made for her company's employees. Other companies were now offering added benefits for domestic partners such as health care, joint loan applications, and beneficiary benefits, just to name a few. She thanked the women for going the distance and said she felt proud to know them.

In April 2006, a prestigious benefit, "Night of 100 Champions" for the Gay Games VII, was held in Chicago. B and Kendall were invited to receive an award and be recognized among one hundred individuals and organizations from the world of sports. Other honorees included leaders in culture, media, community, public service, and business. The award recognized people for bringing about positive change in the world and in society. Kendall and B received the award, along with tennis great Martina Navratilova, Olympic champion Greg Louganis, HBO *Real Sports* broadcaster Mary Carillo, and many more. They were proud and humbled to be included in such an amazing and talented group of people.

Looking back on a legal battle that lasted over seven years, the question the women get most often is why they did it. For them, it's an easy answer—because they could. So often when injustices happen, people don't have the resources, time, money, or courage to take on and fight the status quo. Lucky for B and Kendall, they had all of the above—most of all, the courage to stand up and say, "*No*, you don't get to dismiss us and treat us that way."

The law can work, and injustices can be remedied with time, patience, and perseverance. If you know an injustice is being committed, it is up to you to stand up and correct it, no matter how difficult it may seem. When you stand up for what is right, you help the world move toward equality for all.

PERSONAL SPACE

MARRIAGE

From B: Kendall and I had been together more than fifteen years when we had the opportunity to get married. We had a three-month window to marry in California before we feared Prop 8 would take our rights away in 2008. Our lawsuit helped pave the way for domestic partners to have the right to marry, and we wanted to stand up and be counted.

At first, we wanted a large wedding, but all that got very complicated as my parents still did not approve of my lifestyle. So we kept it simple: We told Kendall's mom and brother, my sister, and two close friends we were going to the theater and asked them to join us. Everyone met at our house and a town car picked us up and drove us to Windansea Beach in La Jolla. Our guests were very confused as we walked along the beach to where a judge and photographer stood greeting us. It was a perfect afternoon. Kendall and I wore all-white outfits that we had purchased in Mykonos the prior year.

When our guests figured out it was a surprise wedding, there were a lot of tears of joy. We shared the vows we had written and it was perfect, elegant, and meaningful—just the way we wanted it. We all went out to dinner and toasted the night away. Three months later, we had a celebration with friends and family at our house with cake and champagne. That was a joyous time in California, because so many gay couples got married in case the laws changed. We attended five weddings during that time. It was an exciting chapter for many of us.

Marrying Kendall was the highlight of my life. We just celebrated thirty years together and have never looked back.

CHAPTER EIGHTEEN

Full Circle

2020

The press release read:

> *FOR IMMEDIATE RELEASE: December 19, 2015. ClubCorp acquires Bernardo Heights Country Club. ClubCorp, a leading owner/operator of private clubs, announced the acquisition of Bernardo Heights Country Club, a private, previously member-owned club located in north county San Diego. ClubCorp planned a multi-million-dollar reinvention project that would bring new dining, social, and family features that would enhance the club experience.*

The Dallas company bought BHCC for an undisclosed amount. ClubCorp is a publicly traded corporation with two-hundred-plus golf and country clubs in its portfolio.

A new sheriff was in town! B and Kendall would never really know how much influence the lengthy legal battle had impacted the financial landscape of BHCC. Everyone would reach their own conclusions. The economy at the time was detrimental to the survival of country club environments across the US—and the negative press BHCC faced during those seven years was immeasurable. Why would anyone join a club that was involved in a discrimination lawsuit? No, the women would never know their impact, but they know that the solution they wanted and had offered from the very beginning would have avoided the entire fiasco.

In October of 2020, a new friend of B's named Brad texted her and invited her to play golf with him at a club he had joined just the month before. She accepted and asked where they would be playing. To her surprise, he texted back: "BHCC." She was totally thrown off guard. She called him to inquire if he knew her history with the club, which he did not. She cautioned him that if she accepted his invitation, he might run into trouble with some members who may still blame her and Kendall for the club's demise and the lawsuit. Brad said he didn't care. B also cautioned him that members could shun him for playing with her. He didn't care. He just wanted to play golf with her, no matter the outcome. He had joined the club with his three buddies, and he would always have them to play with if there were an issue with the existing members.

B accepted the invitation. She was curious what it would be like to go back to the club after thirteen years. She had always really liked the course layout and the proximity to their home, as well as the friendly staff. Much to B's surprise, on the day she and Brad played, word got out very quickly that she had been spotted in the pro shop. Employees who knew her from the past made it a point to come and give her a hug. Three pro shop employees greeted her like a long-lost friend.

It was a great feeling! The staff had always been kind, courteous, friendly, and extremely supportive of Kendall and B. They had gone out of their way to be ultra-attentive to the couple because they knew of the pressure and fury that surrounded them during the lawsuit.

Brad and B played eighteen holes of golf that day without any backlash. Much to B's surprise, the demographic of the membership had totally changed. The pro staff told B that only about 15 percent of the old guard was still there and the rest of the membership was new. That was a shock.

The entire club and golf course looked updated and modern; all improvements having been made by the new ownership. I was delighted to see so much diversity at the club, which was a big change from her previous days at BHCC. The club had also acquired many young members. There was a lot of new energy and B felt right at home. She and Brad shared a drink in the remodeled bar, and over drinks he outlined the current membership drive to attract new members. He had her full attention. It was almost too good to be true!

Since BHCC was no longer an equity club, the monthly dues were less than B had paid for herself alone as an equity member. All that was required was a current member to sponsor her and Kendall, which would also waive the initiation fee. A major bonus was that they would have access to play at two hundred other ClubCorp-owned golf courses, paying only cart fees and a small surcharge. The other courses were spread out across the US—perfect for Kendall and B with their love of travel.

B called Kendall from the car on her way home and gave her all the specifics. Brad had invited them both to play the course the following week, and they gladly accepted. It was a lot of fun and Kendall especially enjoyed the round. This gave B another chance to play the course and see how it felt. They both wondered how much negativity their attendance would create, but there was none. With mostly new members at the club, they blended in nicely. After the round, they had drinks at the bar with many welcoming "hellos" for Kendall from the old staff. In some ways, the women felt as if they had never left. They decided to move forward to see about the potential of becoming members.

The next day, Kendall and B met with the membership adviser and inquired about purchasing a family membership. She was very welcoming. They shared their story about the lawsuit with her and later followed up with a seven-minute video about the case, produced by Equality California. They asked her to share it with the GM and anyone involved with the vetting of new members. They wanted to make sure they disclosed everything about their past and they wanted to play golf together under one membership. Two days later, the membership adviser called and said there would be no problem with them joining. They were overjoyed.

An old friend of B's who joined the club after they left and the lawsuit was settled sponsored them the following week. The couple decided to put the membership in Kendall's name this time, just because they could. It felt very personal to them. Then they got one locker and had both of their names put on it—because they could. Another feel-good moment!

Fifteen years ago, if you had bet B and Kendall a million dollars that they would someday be back at BHCC as members, they would have said, "No way!" But isn't life fascinating? With everything they had gone through—all the time, money, and disappointments—they were right back where they started.

After all, at the end of the day, they just wanted to play golf together.

PERSONAL SPACE

"SCENE OF THE CRIME" PARTY

After the lawsuit was settled and behind us, we hosted a "Scene of the Crime" party/fundraiser at BHCC. We invited one hundred guests for cocktails, dinner, and dancing, and we took over the club that night.

Our honored guests were Jon Davidson and Mary Fechtig. Everyone took turns speaking about the victory we achieved with our seven-year battle for equal rights. We gave Jon and Mary each a Tiffany ring as our appreciation for their contribution to a great cause. Without them, we would not have been there that night celebrating.

That night, we raised $15,000 for Lambda Legal and contributed another $20,000. We danced till midnight, drank cosmos, and celebrated how grateful we were that it was all over. It was a perfect night.

EPILOGUES

2025

B's Epilogue

It has been five years since we started the book and four years since we rejoined the club. The first year, we returned as Associate members, which provided limited access to the golf course. This allowed us to truly assess just how welcome we really were. We are thrilled to say we did not experience any issues or retribution from any of the old members. After that first year, we rejoined as full members.

Now, we are happy to be back where it all began—at the club where I bought the membership for my birthday over thirty years ago. We have reconciled with old friends and made many wonderful new ones. Both of us play on the club's women's golf teams, participate in Member-Guest events, and have been invited by the Golf Professionals to take part in prestigious tournaments, including the four-day Invited (formerly known as ClubCorp) Golf Clubs Invitational. This journey has taken us to incredible places like Palm Beach and Kiawah Island, and we look forward to this year's event at Pinehurst.

When we reflect on the lawsuit and the heartache it caused, we are reminded of the lessons it taught us and the good that ultimately came from it. At its core was simply about fairness, our ability to play golf together, being treated equally, and standing up for what is right. Change does not happen overnight, but it must happen.

We hold no ill will toward anyone. We are all fallible, and it is through recognizing and accepting our own fallibility—as well as that of others—that we can find common ground. During these turbulent times, if conflicts could be approached with compassion, patience, fairness, equality, and heartfelt open-mindedness, our lives would be fuller, more confident, and far more optimistic.

Kendall's Epilogue

It's ladies' day at the club. We just finished a tournament and headed to lunch with all the women. It's been five years since we started the book and four years since we rejoined the club, but as we mingled, chatted, and laughed about our day on the course, there's not even a hint of the lawsuit, the animosity, or the unpleasantness that once surrounded us.

Yes, many of the members here joined after that time, but even among the handful who were part of the club during the height of the ugliness, there's no sign of lingering tension. If you were to observe the luncheon today, you'd never know there was ever an issue. It's like it never happened—in the best possible way.

As the saying goes, time heals all wounds. But healing doesn't happen by itself. You have to be open to it. When we reflect on some of our darkest days—the pain of how we were treated at the club—it's refreshing and humbling to see that everyone involved, including us, has learned how to move forward and let the past stay in the past.

Now, we are fully immersed in club life. We enjoy ladies' day, playing on teams, participating in couples' events and club tournaments, and feeling the warmth and friendliness when we walk into the restaurant or bar after a round of golf. It's a wonderful feeling to be accepted and to feel like we belong in a place that means so much to us.

That said, we can't deny that there are moments when we reflect on the amount of time and energy this ordeal took, and we sometimes question whether it was worth it. The heartache, the legal battles, the emotional toll—it's hard not to wonder. But in the end, we realize that we must all be stewards of change. Anything worth having is worth fighting for.

We created this opportunity for ourselves because, twenty years ago, we weren't willing to accept anything less. We fought for our place and had the patience to wait for others to catch up, to grow comfortable with true acceptance. Looking back now, we know it was the right thing to do.

ACKNOWLEDGMENTS

A very special thank-you to the following friends and family that without them our victory would not have been possible.

Jeff O'Connor

Mary Fechtig

Jim McElroy

Truth French

Gabriele Zimmerman

Logan Jenkins

Elizabeth Polachok-Belland

Martha Lawrence

Colette Carlson

Scott Shellstrom

HBO *Real Sports*

Osher Lifelong Learning Institute,
UCSD San Diego Writing Class of 2020

B. Birgit Koebke (left) and Kendall E. French

ABOUT THE AUTHORS

B. BIRGIT KOEBKE was born in Bremen, Germany, in 1956—first-generation German. She immigrated to the US from Germany when she was in fifth grade, after having lived in Santiago, Chile, for two years in grades two through four. She has a BA in business and an MA in counseling. B spent the majority of her career selling advertising, starting with print advertising and radio. She then moved to television and worked at CBS 8 in San Diego as a senior account executive for thirty-six years. She speaks fluent German and has a good understanding of Spanish. B loves travel, the ocean, golf, and skiing. B lives by the principles "Fun is first" and "Work hard and play harder," and always remembers that, in life, there are no shortcuts.

KENDALL FRENCH is a native Californian who grew up in Laguna Beach. After graduating from San Diego State University with a BA in public administration, she decided to make San Diego her home and pursue her passion for the hotel business. She joined Marriott Hotels where she spent the next fifteen years in hotel convention sales. Kendall dabbled in the dot-com and automotive industries for several years before landing her dream job as a sales rep for GlaxoSmithKline Pharmaceuticals. Over the next fourteen years, Kendall rose through the ranks, retiring from GSK as a district sales manager. Kendall's passions are cooking, mixology, and entertaining family and friends. She stays active as an avid golfer, skier, and cyclist.

B and Kendall have been together thirty-two years. They live in San Diego with their two Chihuahuas, Patron and Mavrik.

www.ingramcontent.com/pod-product-compliance
Lightning Source LLC
LaVergne TN
LVHW090412210926
848480LV00002B/545
9798992643206